AF580012

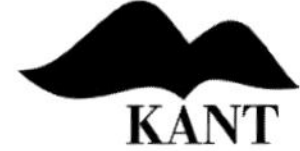
KANT

erwin staeheli

PASSAGE

Introduction

Particular images are stuck in my memory. For example: footprints in the black, rain-sodden soil and young blackberry shoots creeping over the ground. And shreds of white plastic on broken branches along the edge of a highway. A gap in the undergrowth, a narrow, thorny passage, beyond, a field of neglected fruit trees. A few men are crouching on camping chairs and wooden crates. They are hardly identifiable in the pale morning light. The figures are staring at the ground in front of them seemingly unaware of my presence. The area is surrounded by a wall containing a half-open iron doorway. It leads to a dark passage with more doors leading to abandoned rooms. Mattresses, clothes and suitcases lie scattered. At the end of the gloomy corridor is the entrance to an empty warehouse: all concrete walls and no exit anywhere, just gaps high in the walls through which the bright, colourless sky is visible.

The most puzzling object I had found in an abandoned house is an overseas trunk filled with chaff. Quite likely it can still be found, labelled "Buenos Aires", in the cellar of a Tuscan farmhouse. Presumably this piece of luggage had arrived in Buenos Aires by sea via Italy and was later returned. The trunk reminds me of my grandfather. He had emigrated to Argentina in the year 1920. For weeks he was shovelling coal on a steamship to pay for his passage. The stokers were forbidden to go up on the deck. He therefore never came face to face with the ocean. In Argentina he intended to grow acacia trees to trade the wood for tool handles. He was defrauded during the purchase of his land, lost all his savings and decided to return home the same way he had arrived.

In our family one never mentioned my grandfather's travels. I remember a well-thumbed Spanish dictionary: it resided on the old man's desk. In his garden in Switzerland he planted some thorny robinias, also known as false acacias, next to his fruit trees. After my grandfather had passed away the trees were chopped down but new shoots kept growing from the root system and stubbornly refused to be eradicated.

Passage: a few words about the pictures in the book. Whilst inhabited rooms are furnished to fulfil a specific purpose for the user, this function falls away with unoccupied and unused rooms. The point of these rooms is limited, they exist only to be walked through or to be given a brief glance. The passages are familiar enough to settle in to only a few: maybe beggars or street buskers in underground pedestrian passageways. The few objects scattered around look lost. They are without meaning and worth. Passages do not invite prolonged lingering, especially when they are exposed to the draught. In passages one gets the feeling to be away from where one wanted to leave from and having not yet arrived at where one wants to go.

One phenomenon is particularly interesting, namely the play of light: when light enters gloomy spaces it gets lost within and creates in us a strong desire to know its source, and to find it immediately. One is seized by a kind of yearning. As there is not much holding us back one spontaneously strives towards this goal. One becomes active. This is completely different from lived-in rooms where one would take a seat on a chair or lie in a bed and would therefore become motionless.

The images from "Passage" show mainly mundane locations: underground pedestrian passageways, factories, hotels, highway-tunnels. As a rule everything is dirty. I dislike discarded litter and defaced walls. These cultural marks disturb the simple structure of the buildings. They feel aggressive. I understand the fear of empty spaces and rooms. It is tempting to leave behind tags and traces. But it is the filth that disturbs the tranquillity of these places.

Passages and empty rooms can be dangerous. This does not particularly concern me. Sometimes, thanks to the usual CCTV cameras, I am spotted by security guards. "What are you doing here?" they call out to me. Then no explanation helps. My response is rarely accepted.

Some places can have a menacing effect on me. My inner turmoil comes from the rooms when they reflect my own world of deficient memories. In passages, therefore transitory spaces, traces of the past gradually vanish because nobody cares about the state of the construction. These places are not deemed worthy enough to be safeguarded. And I wouldn't blame anybody for it. Painted tags and loose items disappear the quickest. The empty shell still shows the purpose of the building. But then the structure crumbles. I react to this decay by suppressing my instinct to flee, by observing the play of light, listening to the noises, smelling wet mortar and concrete, caressing naked walls in the semi-darkness, following trails in the dust....and sometimes taking a photograph.

The second stage of the finished picture happens in the laboratory. The darkroom is a peaceful and familiar place. Here the images emerge slowly in the developer solution. I discover traces and objects that I had not been aware of at the time. The film sees more than my eyes. By enlarging the photograph and increasing the contrast unrecognised images appear. Sometimes I have a strong desire to return to the place where I had shot the picture. This is not always possible. So there is nothing for it but to admire the new discovery in the picture without being able to verify its existence in reality.

Úvod

V paměti mi utkvěly určité obrazy. Třeba šlépěje v černé, deštěm promočené půdě, po níž se plazí mladé výhonky ostružin. Cáry bílých plastových fólií na polámaných větvích stromů podél dálnice. Díra v podrostu, úzký, trnitý průchod ze sadu se zanedbanými ovocnými stromy. Několik mužů shrbeně sedí na kempingových židlích a dřevěných bednách. Sotva je lze rozeznat v bledém ranním světle. Postavy zírají na zem před sebou, aniž by si uvědomovaly mou přítomnost. Místo je obehnáno zdí, v níž je pootevřená železná brána. Vede k temnému průchodu s mnoha dveřmi k opuštěným místnostem. Jsou v nich rozházené matrace, součásti oděvu, kufry. Na konci tmavé chodby je vstup do prázdného skladu: všude kolem betonové zdi a žádný východ, jen úzké díry vysoko ve zdi, kterými proniká bledé světlo bezbarvé oblohy.

Nejzáhadnější předmět, který jsem v opuštěném domě našel, byl veliký lodní kufr naplněný plevami. Takové kufry s nálepkou "Buenos Aires" lze stále ještě nalézt ve sklepích toskánských statků. Asi se dostal do Buenos Aires po moři z Itálie a později se vrátil zpět. Kufr mě připomíná mého dědečka. Emigroval do Argentíny v roce 1920. Týdny házel uhlí do kotle na parníku, aby tak zaplatil za cestu. Topiči měli zakázáno chodit na palubu, nikdy tedy nespatřil oceán. V Argentíně chtěl pěstovat akáty a prodávat jejich dřevo na topůrka a násady. Při koupi půdy byl podveden, přišel o všechny své úspory a rozhodl se vrátit domů stejným způsobem, jakým přijel. V naší rodině nikdo o cestách mého dědečka nemluvil. Pamatuji se na ohmataný španělský slovník, ležel stále na jeho stole. Ve své zahradě ve Švýcarsku vysadil vedle ovocných stromů pár trnovníků, kterým se také říká falešné akáty. Poté, co dědeček zemřel, byly stromy vykáceny, ale z kořenů stále vyrůstaly nové výhonky a vzpurně odolávaly vymýcení.

Průchody - pár slov o fotografiích v knize: Zatímco obydlené prostory jsou zařízeny tak, aby splňovaly svůj účel pro uživatele, u neobývaných prostor tomu tak není. Jejich smysl je omezen, slouží jen jako průchody nebo jako objekty letmého pohledu. Pocit blízké důvěrnosti tam najde málokdo a snad proto se v podchodech k metru usazují jen žebráci či pouliční muzikanti. Věci tam vypadají, jako by je někdo ztratil. Nemají žádný smysl ani hodnotu. Průchody nezvou k delšímu setrvání, zvláště když je v nich průvan. Často v nich máte pocit, že jste už odešli z místa, kde jste nechtěli být, ale dosud nenašli to pravé.

Zvláště zajímavá je hra světla v průchodech: v temných prostorách se světlo ztrácí, a proto se okamžitě snažíme najít jeho zdroj. Člověk je při tom zasažen nezkrotnou touhou. A protože nás nic nedrží, spontánně směřujeme k tomuto cíli. Začneme být aktivní. To se naprosto liší od pocitů v obytných prostorách, kde by se člověk nejraději posadil do křesla anebo položil do postele a nehnul se z místa.

Fotografie v „Průchodech" pocházejí z reálného světa: zobrazují podchody v metru, továrny, hotely, dálniční tunely. Zpravidla jsou všechna ta místa špinavá. Nemám rád rozházené odpadky a počmárané zdi. Projevy této kultury narušují jednoduchou strukturu budov. Ty pak působí agresivně. Chápu strach z prázdných prostor a místností. Je to lákavé zanechávat po sobě své tagy a kresby. Ale je to špína, která narušuje poklidnost těchto míst.

Průchody a prázdné prostory mohou být nebezpečné. Nějak zvlášť mě to neznepokojuje. Zásluhou všudypřítomných CCTV kamer si mě někdy všimnou hlídači. „Co tady děláte?" křičí na mě. Žádná vysvětlení zde nepomáhají. Zřídka kdy je přijmou.

V některých místech se cítím ohrožen. Můj vnitřní rozruch vychází z míst, která rezonují s mým vlastním světem nejasných vzpomínek. V průchodech, jež jsou pomíjivými prostorami, stopy minulosti postupně mizí, protože se nikdo nestará o stav těchto staveb. Tato místa se nepokládají za tak hodnotná, aby jim byla poskytována ochrana. Nedávám to nikomu za vinu. Nejrychleji mizejí kresby a ty části, které se snadno uvolní. Holá kostra stále ještě naznačuje původní účel stavby. Ale pak se její struktura začne drolit. Reaguji na tento rozpad potlačováním vnitřního nutkání k útěku, pozorováním hry světla, nasloucháním různým zvukům, vnímáním vůně vlhké omítky a betonu, dotýkáním se holých stěn v polotmě, sledováním stop v prachu...a někdy také fotografováním.

Druhá fáze tvorby fotografií probíhá v laboratoři. Temná komora je klidné, důvěrně známé místo. V roztoku vývojky zde obrazy pomalu vystupují z nicoty. Objevují se stopy a objekty, kterých jsem si při fotografování nevšiml. Na filmu je toho víc, než zahlédly mé oči. Zvětšením fotografie a zvýšením kontrastu se objevují dosud nerozpoznané detaily obrazů. Někdy mě zachvátí silná touha vrátit se na místo, kde jsem pořídil snímek. Není to vždy možné. Pak mi nezbývá nic jiného, než obdivovat svůj nový objev na fotografii, aniž bych si ověřil jeho existenci ve skutečnosti.

Einleitung

Besondere Bilder bleiben mir in der Erinnerung haften. Zum Beispiel Fußabdrücke in schwarznasser Erde, über die sich junge Brombeerranken vortasten. Und weisse Plastikfetzen an abgebrochenen Ästen entlang einer Schnellstrasse. Ein Loch im Dickicht eines Gestrüpps, ein enger Durchgang mit Dornen, dahinter eine Wiese mit verwilderten Obstbäumen. Im weissen Morgenlicht sind Männer zu erkennen, die auf Campingstühlen oder Kisten hocken. Die Gestalten starren vor sich auf den Boden und scheinen mich nicht wahrzunehmen. Das Grundstück wird begrenzt von einer Mauer mit einer halboffenen Eisentür. Sie führt in einen dunklen Korridor mit weiteren Türen zu verlassenen Räumen. Matratzen, Kleider und Koffer liegen verstreut herum. Am Ende des dunklen Korridors ist der Eingang zu einer leeren Lagerhalle: Ringsum Betonwände und nirgends ein Ausgang, bloss oben in den Wänden Öffnungen, durch die der farblose, sehr helle Himmel zu sehen ist.

Der rätselhafteste Gegenstand, den ich in einem verlassenen Haus gefunden habe ist ein Überseekoffer, gefüllt mit Weizenstreu. Er steht wohl immer noch im Keller eines toskanischen Bauernhauses und trägt die Aufschrift "Buenos Aires". Vermutlich ist das Gepäckstück auf dem Seeweg von Italien nach Buenos Aires gelangt und später wieder zurück geschickt worden. Der Koffer erinnert mich an meinen Grossvater. Er emigrierte im Jahr 1920 nach Argentinien. Wochenlang schaufelte er Kohle in einem Dampfer, um sich das Geld für die Überfahrt zu sparen. Es war den Heizern verboten, an Deck zu gehen. Das Meer bekam er dadurch nie zu Gesicht. In Argentinien versuchte er eine Akazienplantage anzulegen und das Holz für Werkzeugstiele zu verkaufen. Er wurde beim Landkauf betrogen, verlor sein gespartes Geld und beschloss, auf die gleiche Art wieder heimzukehren wie er hergekommen war.

In unserer Familie wurde nie über die Reise meines Grossvaters gesprochen. Ich erinnere mich an ein abgegriffenes spanisches Wörterbuch: Es lag immer auf dem Pult des alten Mannes. In seinem Garten in der Schweiz pflanzte er neben den Fruchtbäumen dornige Robinien, auch "falsche Akazien" genannt. Sie vermehrten sich über die Wurzeltriebe und waren auch lange, nachdem mein Grossvater gestorben war, nicht auszurotten.

Passage. Ein paar Worte zu den Bildern des Buches: Während bewohnte Räume so eingerichtet werden, dass die Benützer bequem leben können, fällt diese Zweckbestimmung bei unbewohnten oder unbenutzten Räumen weg. Der Sinn dieser Räume beschränkt sich darauf, dass man durch sie hindurchgeht oder kurz hineinblickt. Nur Wenigen sind diese Passagen so vertraut, dass sie sich darin niederlassen. Etwa Bettler oder Strassenmusikanten in Fussgängerunterführungen. Die wenigen Gegenstände, die herum liegen, wirken verloren. Sie sind ohne Bedeutung und Wert. Passagen laden nicht dazu ein, sich lange darin aufzuhalten, besonders wenn sie der Zugluft ausgesetzt sind. In Passagen hat man das Gefühl, bereits fort zu sein, von wo man fort gehen wollte und noch nicht dort zu sein, wo man hingehen will.

Ein Phänomen ist besonders interessant, nämlich die Lichtspiele: Dringt Licht in düstere Räume, verliert es sich darin und löst Sehnsucht nach dessen Quelle aus, die man sofort erkunden möchte. Man wird wie von einem Sog erfasst. Da es nicht viel gibt, das einem zurückhält, wird man spontan auf dieses Ziel zustreben. Man kommt in Bewegung. Das ist ganz anders als in bewohnten Räumen, wo man sich auf einen Stuhl setzt oder in ein Bett legt und damit bewegungslos wird.

Die Bilder von "Passage" zeigen meist profane Orte: Fussgängerunterführungen, Fabriken, Hotels, Strassentunnels. Alles ist meistens schmutzig. Ich mag hingeworfenen Abfall und bemalte Wände nicht. Diese kulturellen Spuren stören die einfachen Formen der Gebäude. Sie wirken aggressiv und stören die Ruhe an diesen Orten. Ich verstehe die Angst vor leeren Flächen und Räumen. Es ist verlockend Zeichen und Spuren zu hinterlassen. Manchmal stehen Namen an den Wänden.

Passagen und leere Räume können gefährlich sein. Das stört mich nicht besonders. Wegen der üblichen Überwachungskameras werde ich manchmal von Wächtern ertappt. "Was tun Sie hier?", rufen sie mir zu. Da helfen keine Erklärungen. Meine Antwort wird selten akzeptiert.

Die Orte können bedrohlich auf mich wirken. Die Irritation geht von den Räumen aus, wenn sie meine eigene lückenhafte Erinnerungswelt spiegeln. In Passagen, also Durchgangsräumen, lösen sich Spuren der Vergangenheit auf, weil sich niemand um sie kümmert. Oder die Orte werden nicht wertvoll genug eingeschätzt, sie zu erhalten. Bemalungen, Schriftzeichen und lose Gegenstände verschwinden am schnellsten. Die leere Hülle zeugt noch vom Zweck des Bauwerks. Aber dann brechen die Baumaterialien auseinander. Ich reagiere auf diese Zerfallserscheinungen, indem ich den Instinkt zu fliehen unterdrücke, die Lichtspiele beobachte, auf Geräusche horche, nassen Stein, Mörtel, Beton rieche, im Halbdunkel nackte Wände abtaste, Spuren im Staub folge...und manchmal ein Foto mache.

Der zweite Schritt zum fertigen Bild geschieht im Labor. Die "Dunkelkammer" ist ein ruhiger und vertrauter Ort. Hier tauchen die Bilder langsam aus dem Entwicklungsbad auf. Ich entdecke Spuren und Gegenstände, welche ich vor Ort nicht erkannt hatte: Der Film sieht mehr als mein Auge. Das Vergrössern der Bilder und das Steigern der Kontraste bringt Unerkanntes zutage und ich wünsche mir manchmal, an den Ort der Aufnahmen zurückzukehren. Das ist nicht immer möglich. Es bleibt dann nichts anderes übrig, als die Neuentdeckungen auf dem Bild zu bestaunen, ohne sie in der Wirklichkeit bestätigt zu sehen.

*Il me semble que je serais toujours bien là où je ne suis pas,
et cette question de déménagement
en est une que je discute sans cesse avec mon âme.*

*I have the impression that I would always be comfortable there where I am not,
and this question of moving about is one I am constantly discussing with my soul.*

*Mám pocit, že budu spokojený jen tam, kde právě nejsem,
a otázka pohybu z místa na místo neustále zneklidňuje mou duši.*

*Mir scheint, es würde mir immer dort gut gehen, wo ich nicht bin,
und diese Frage der Veränderung des Wohnsitzes gehört zu denen,
über die ich mit meiner Seele unablässig diskutiere.*

Charles Baudelaire
Le Spleen de Paris
Any where out of the world
Pařížský splín; kdekoliv, daleko od světa

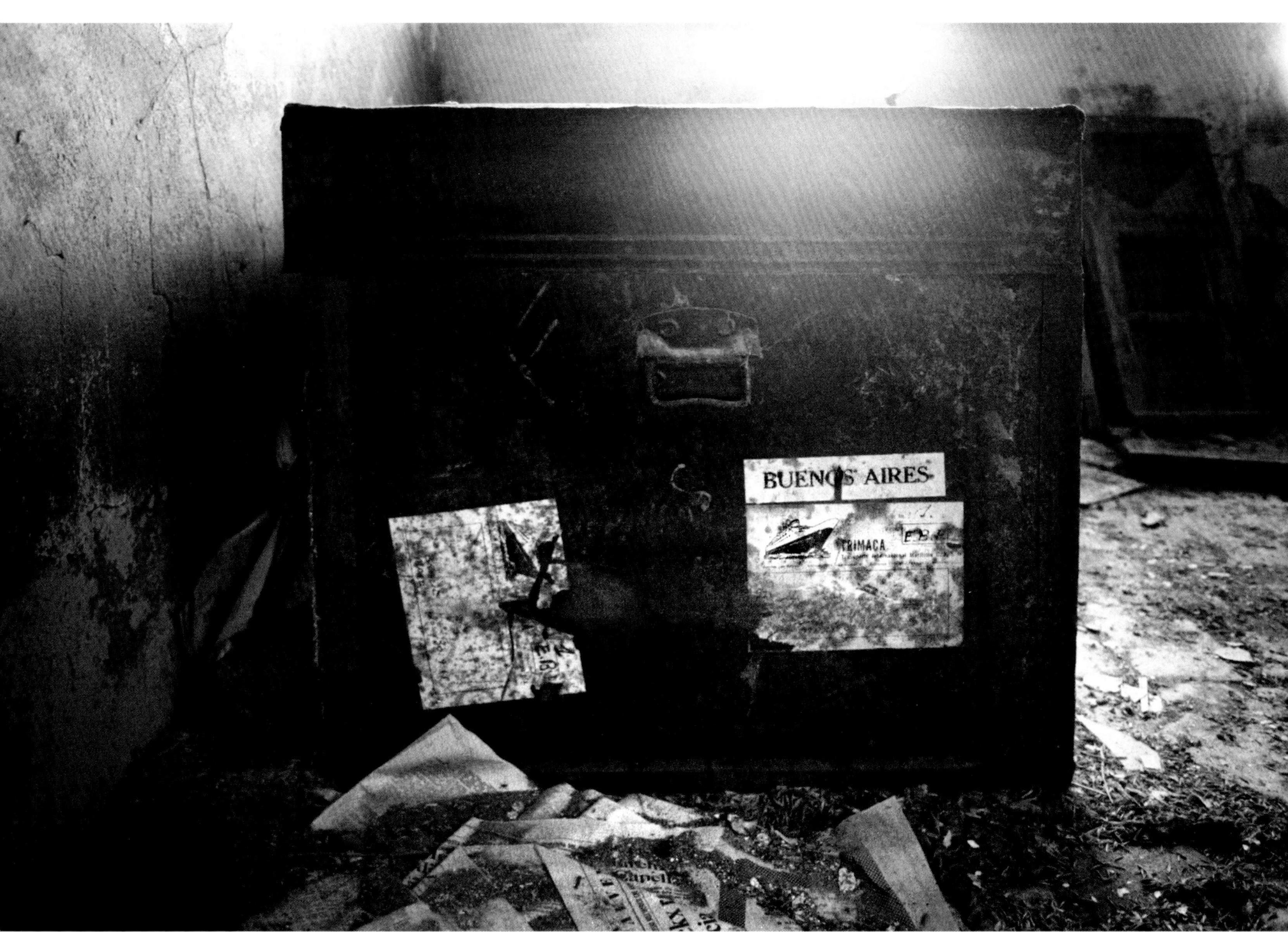
BUENOS AIRES
TRIMACA

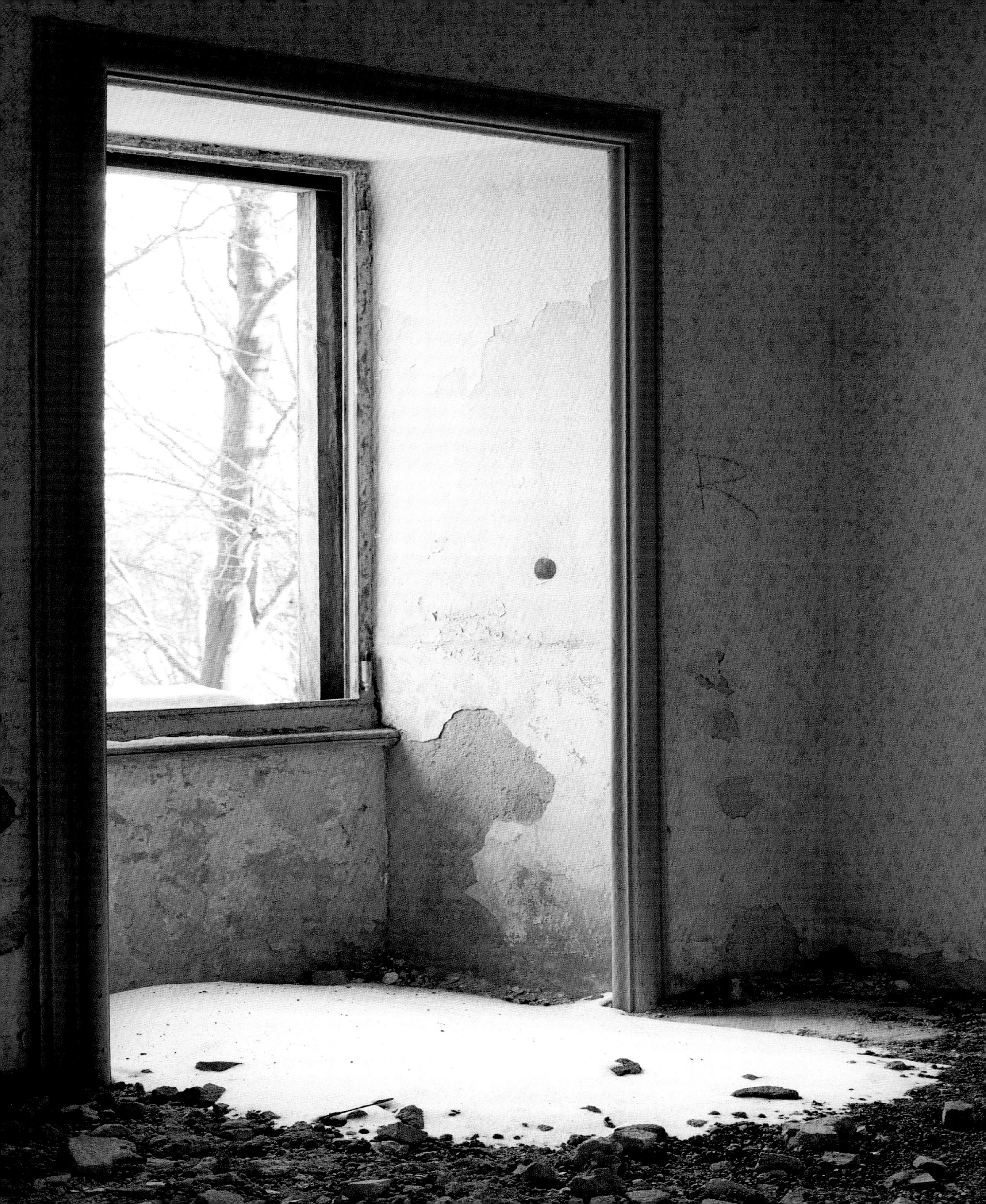

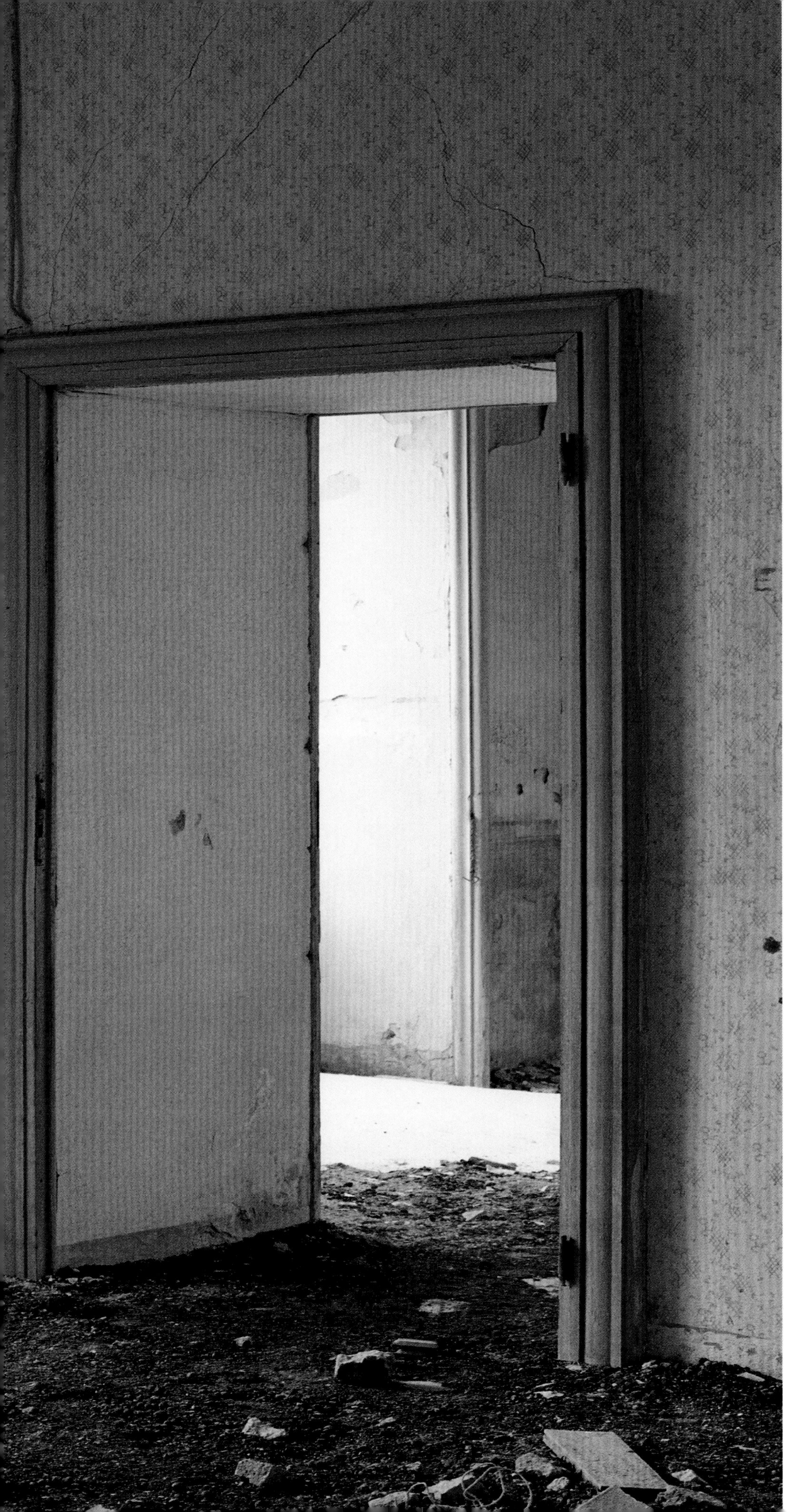

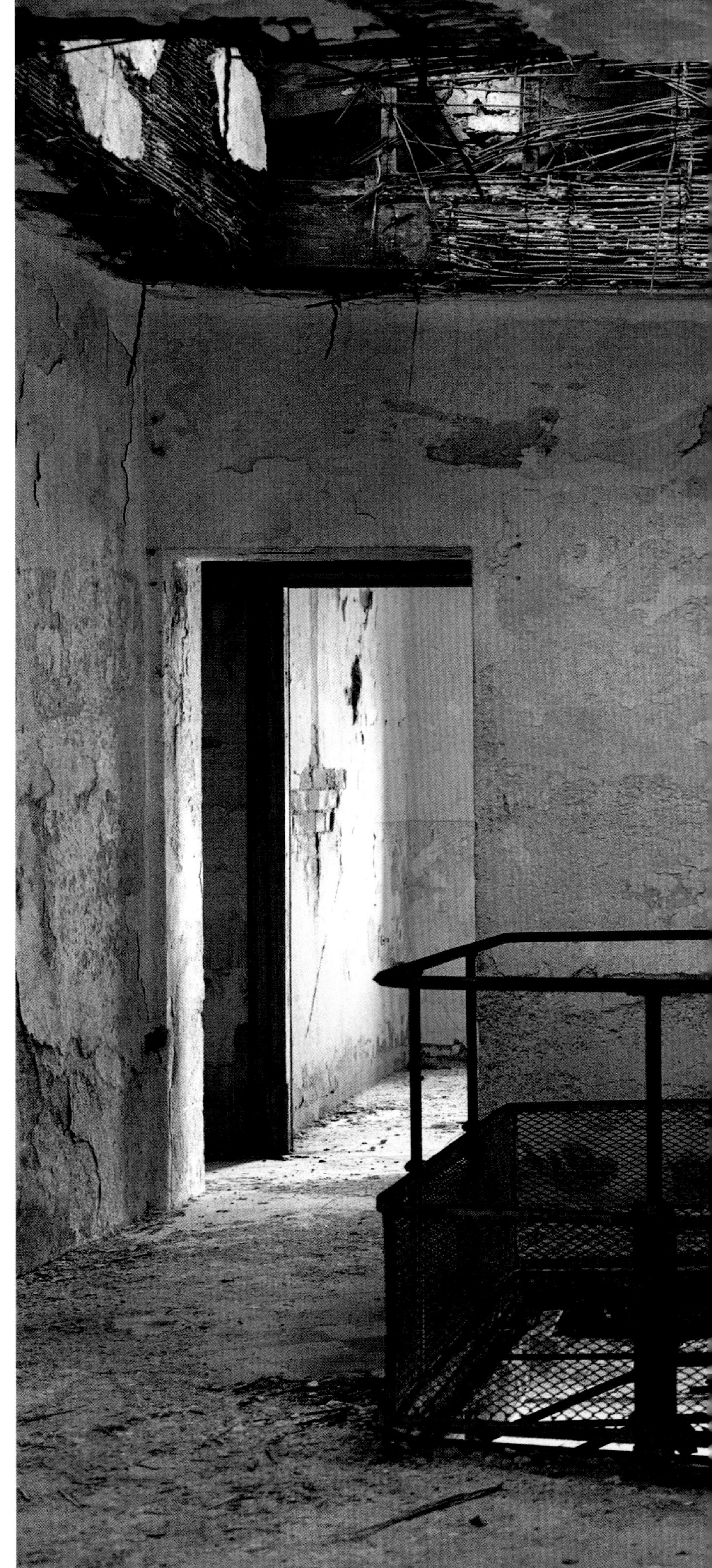

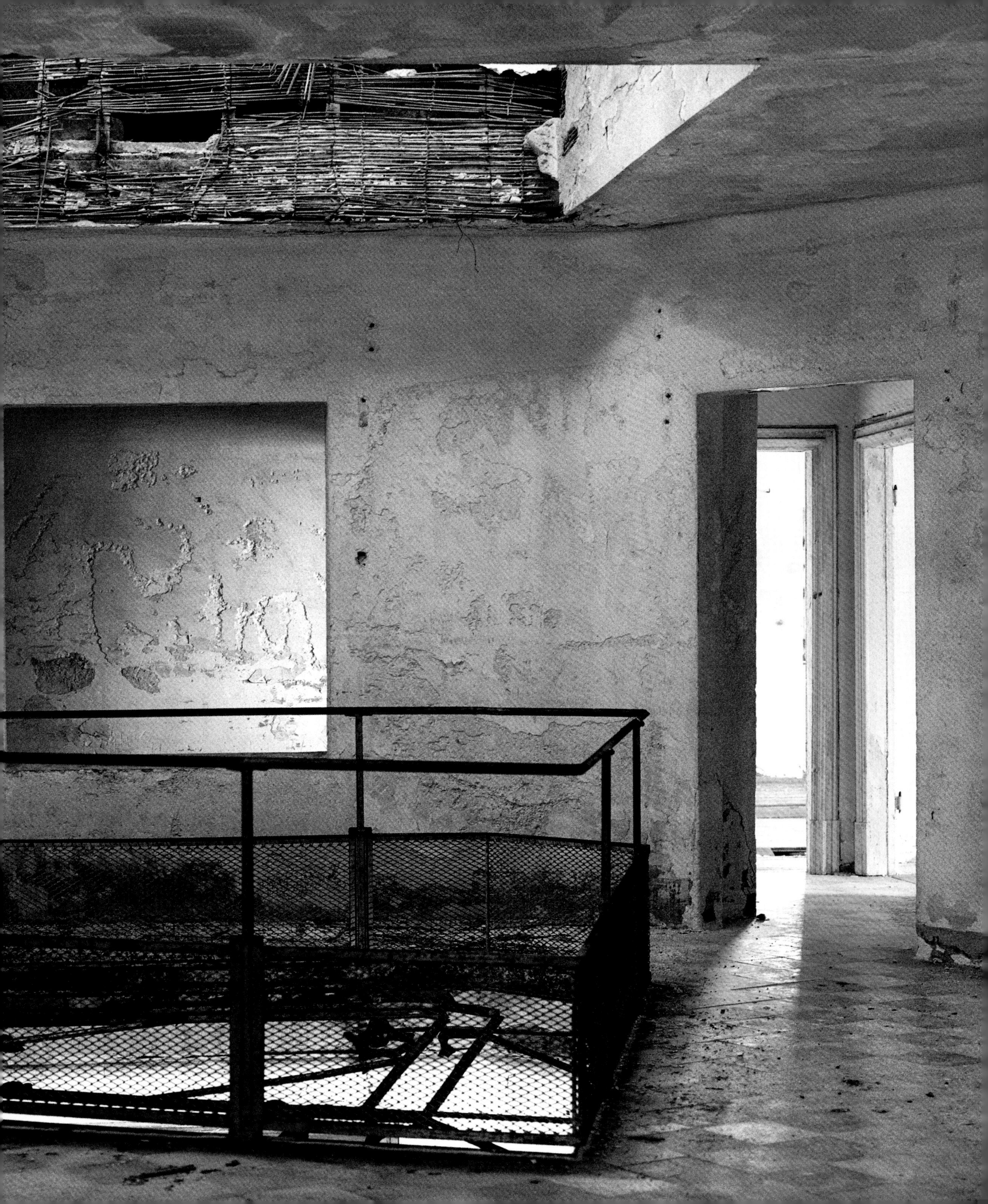

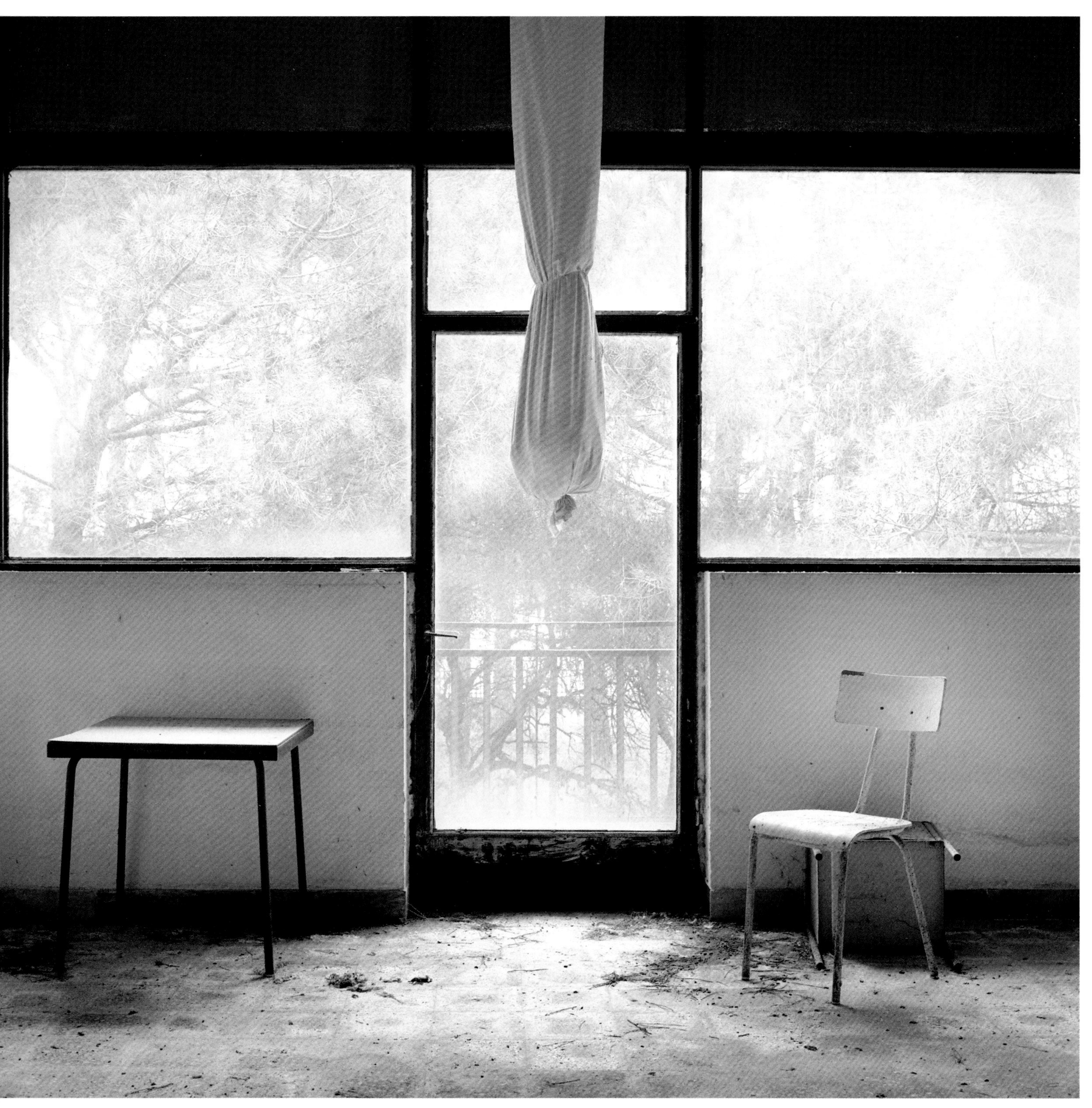

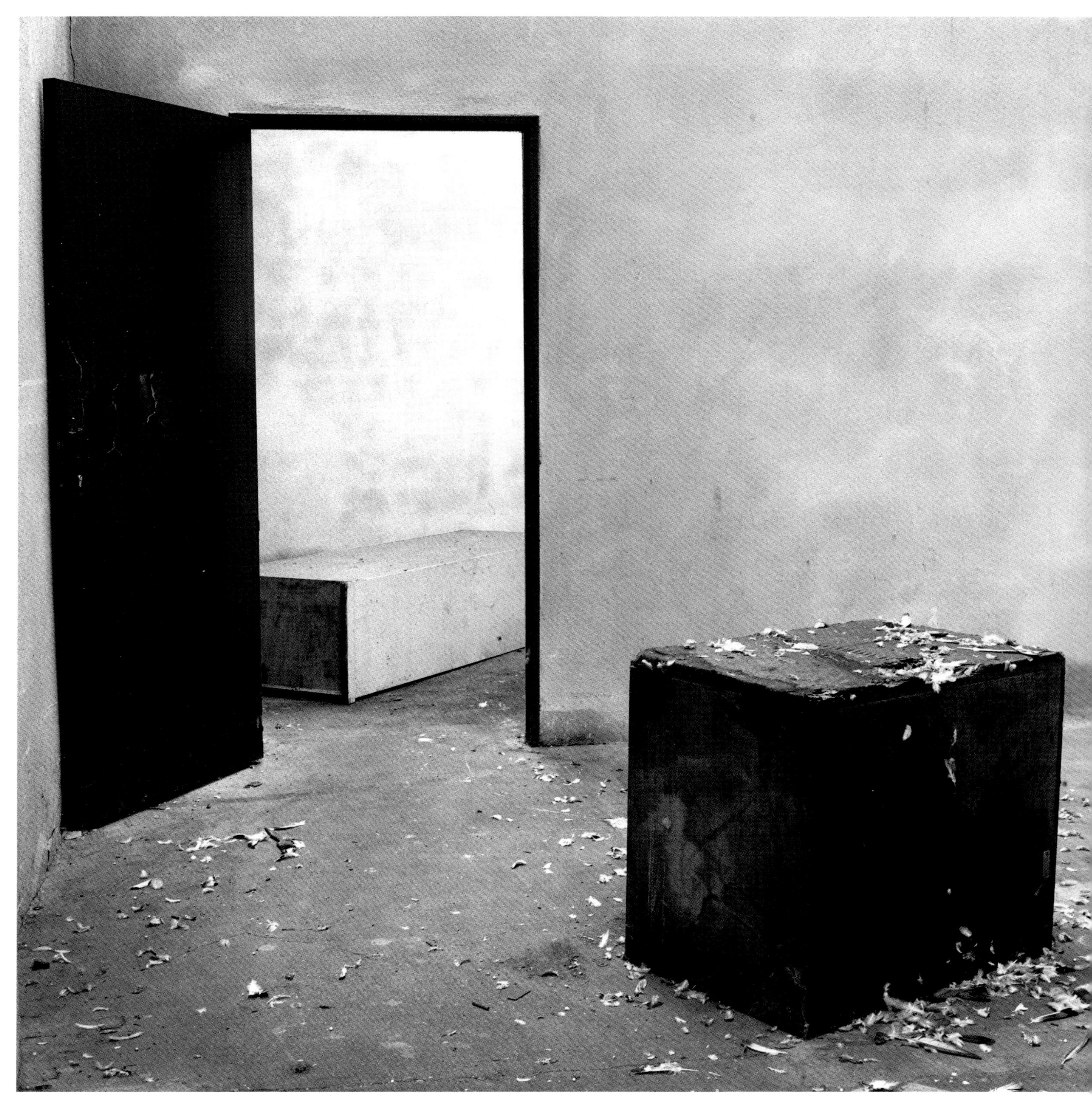

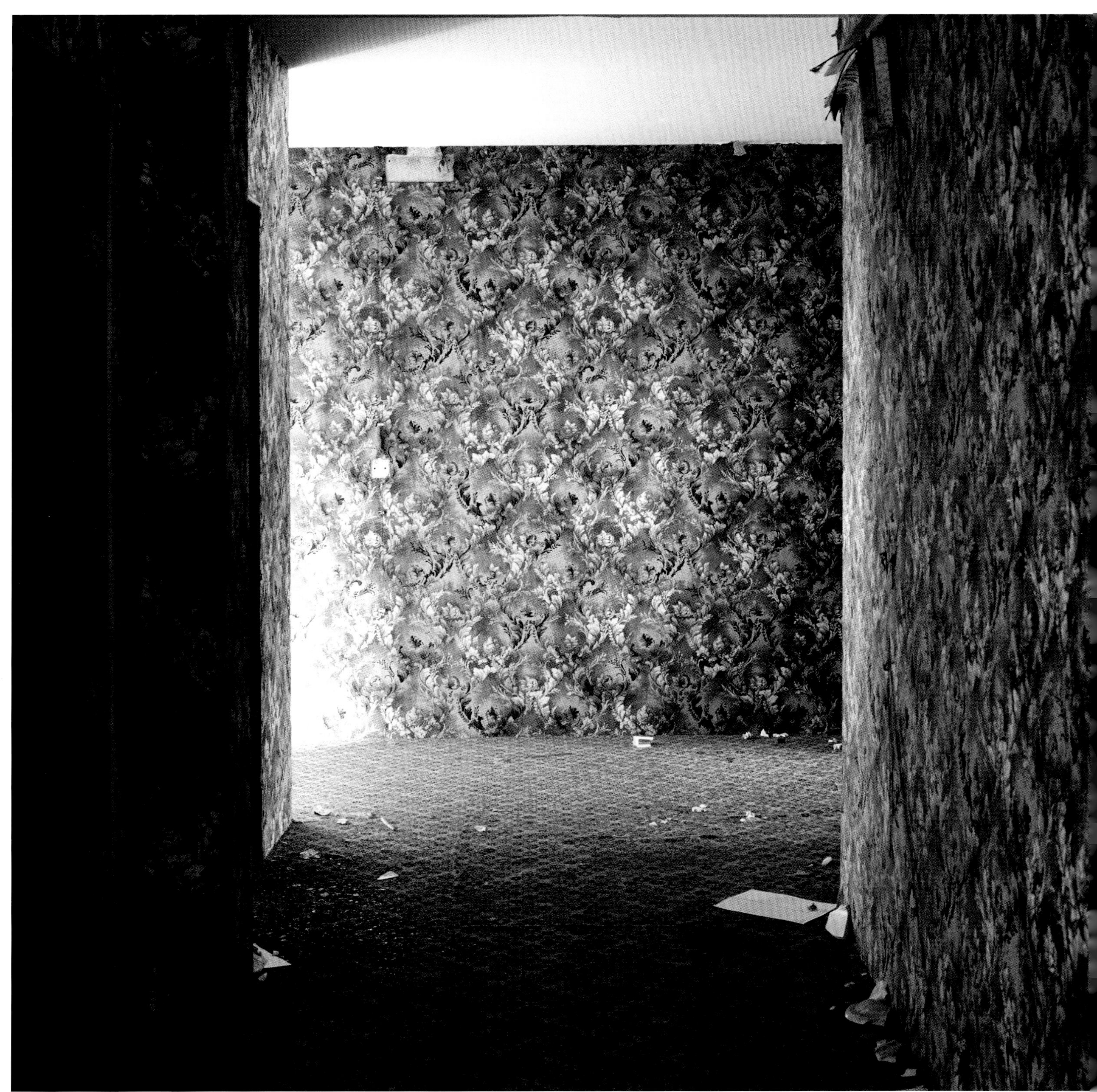

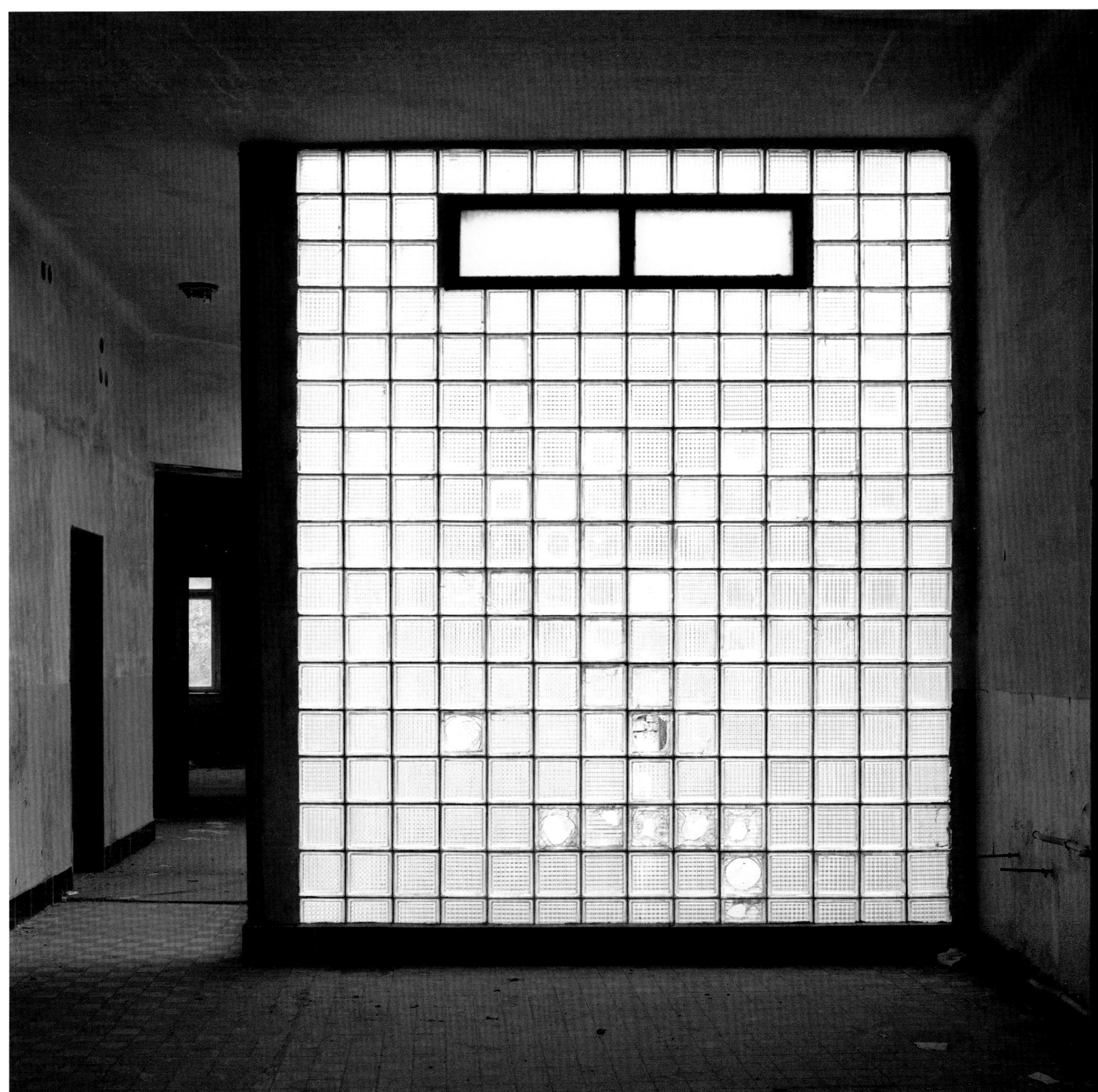

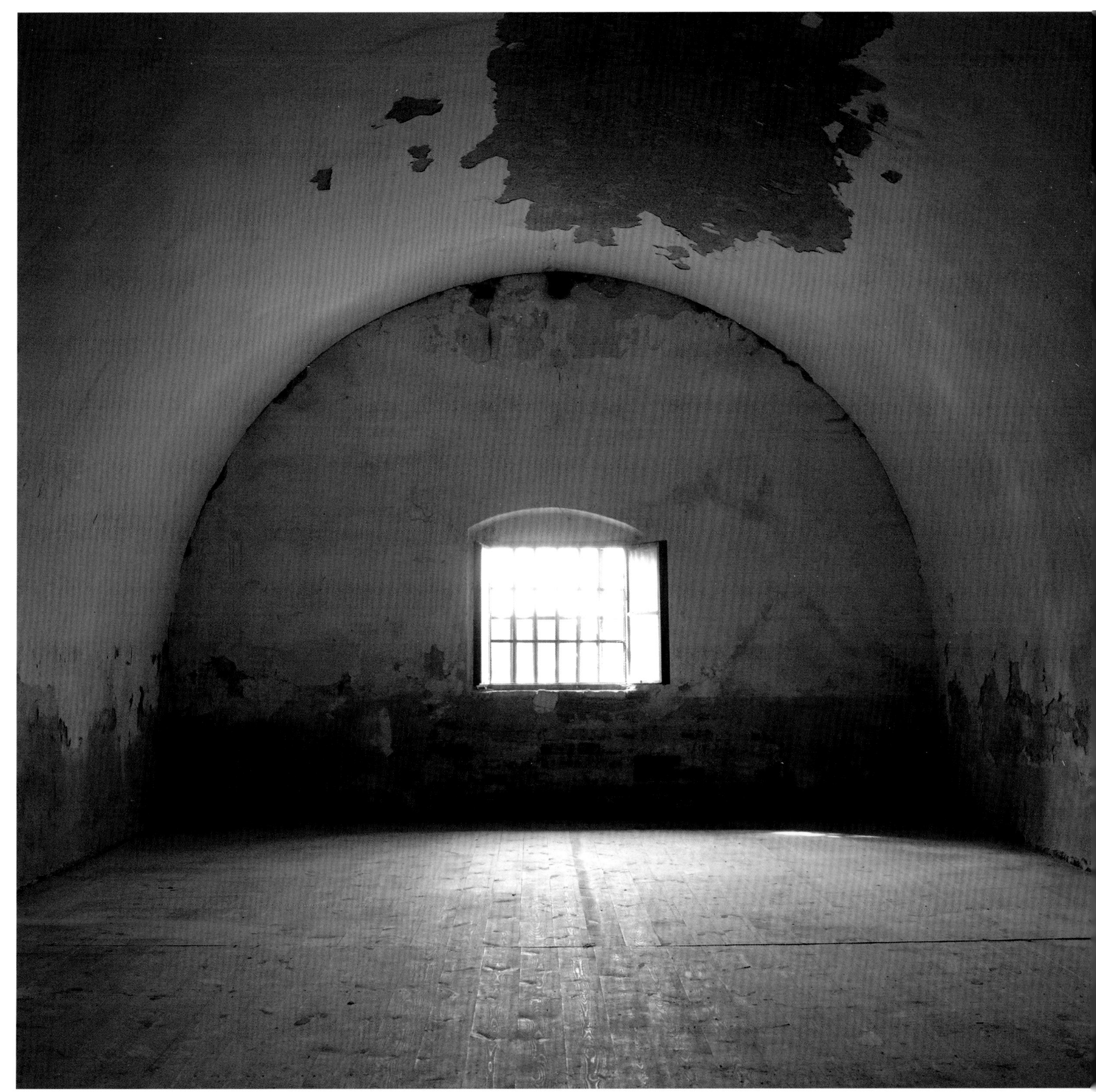

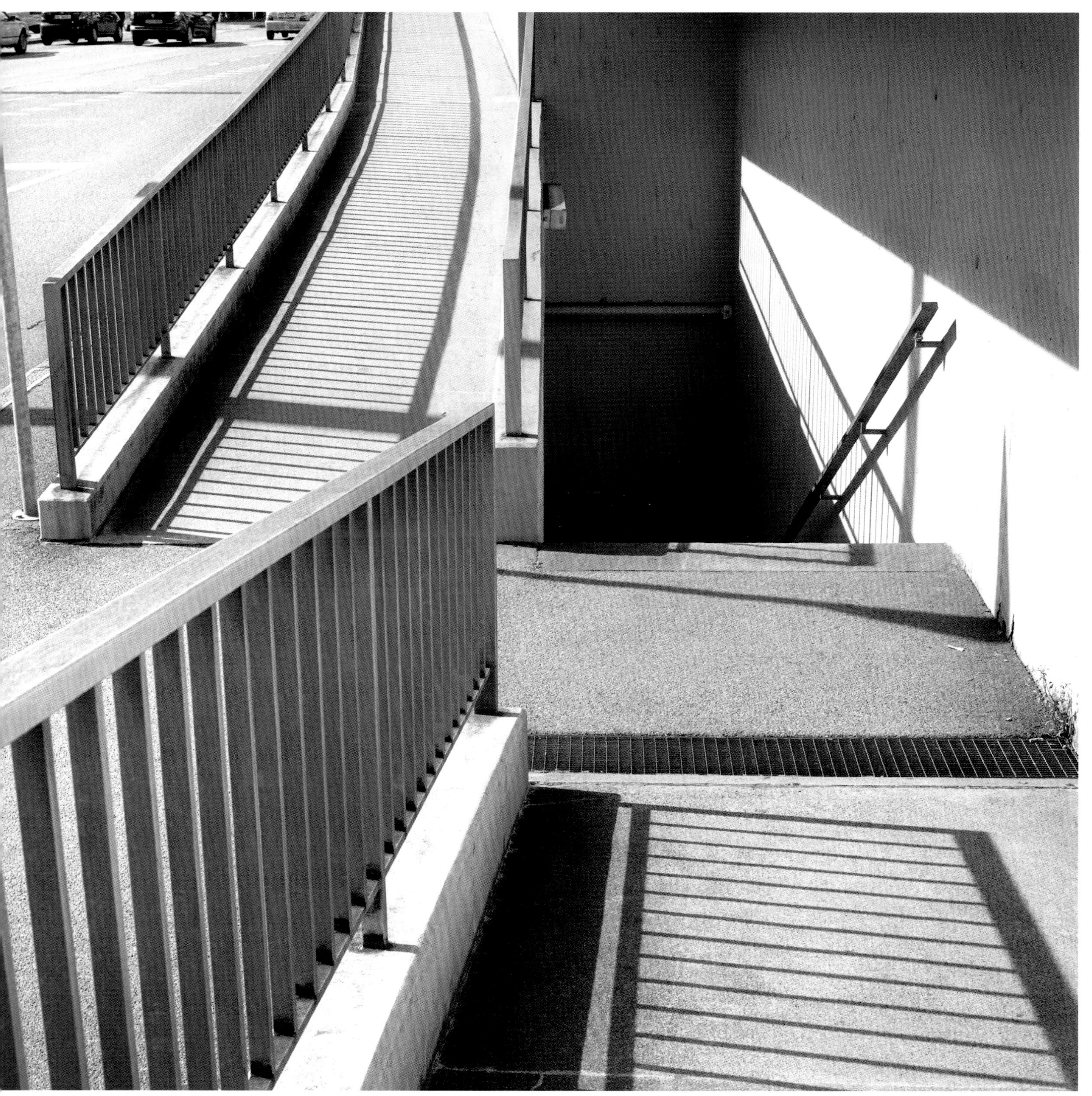

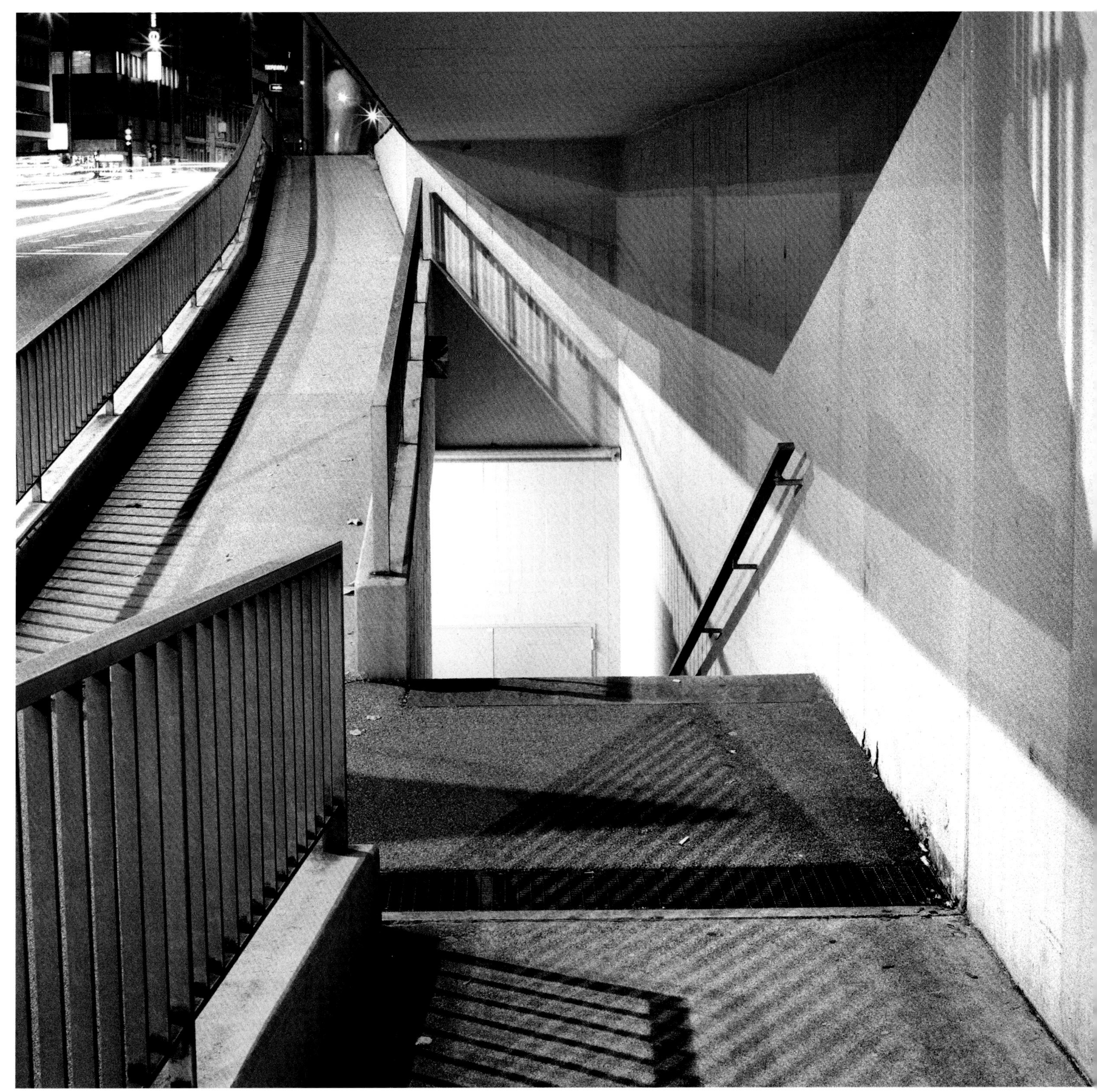

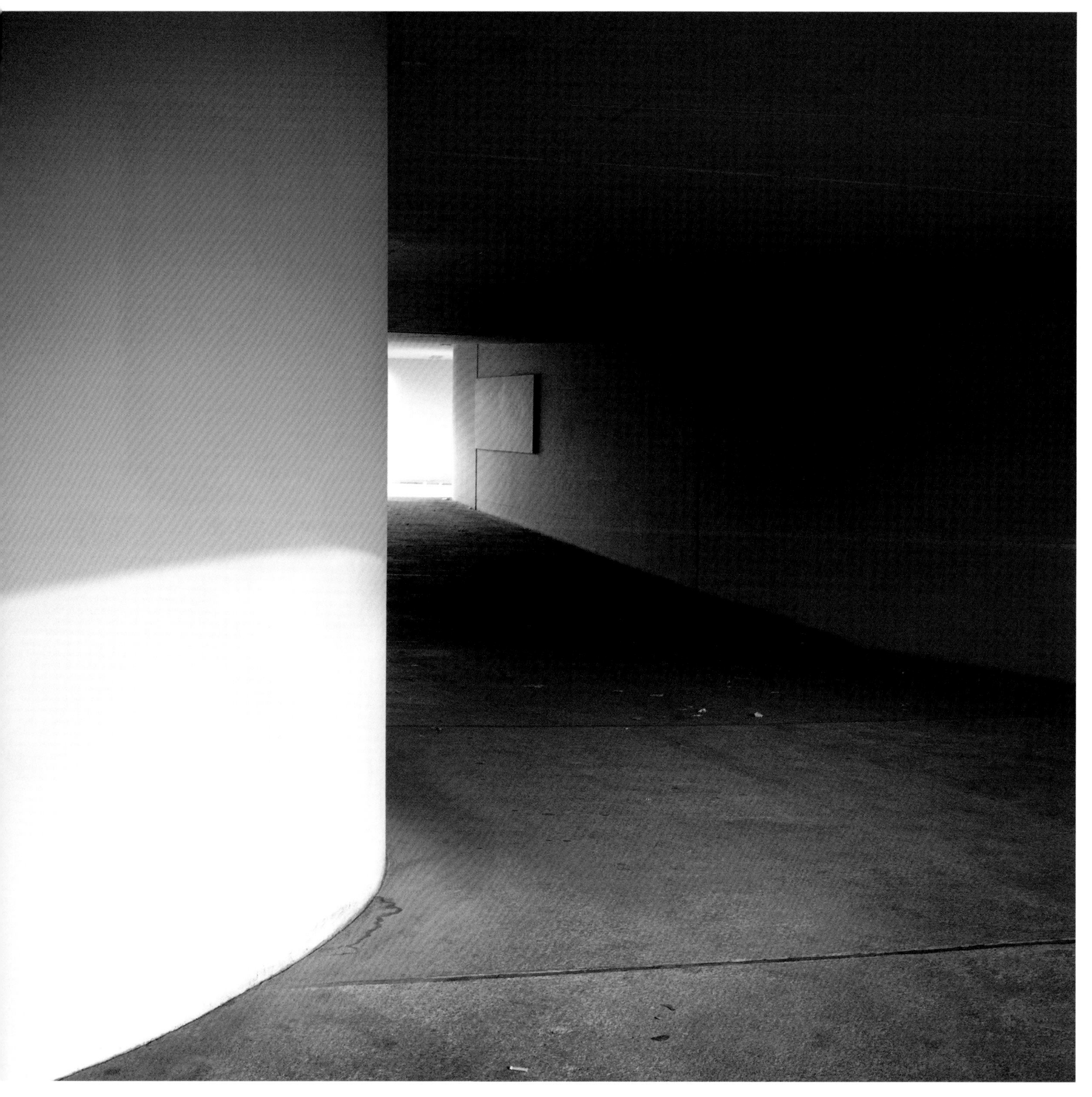

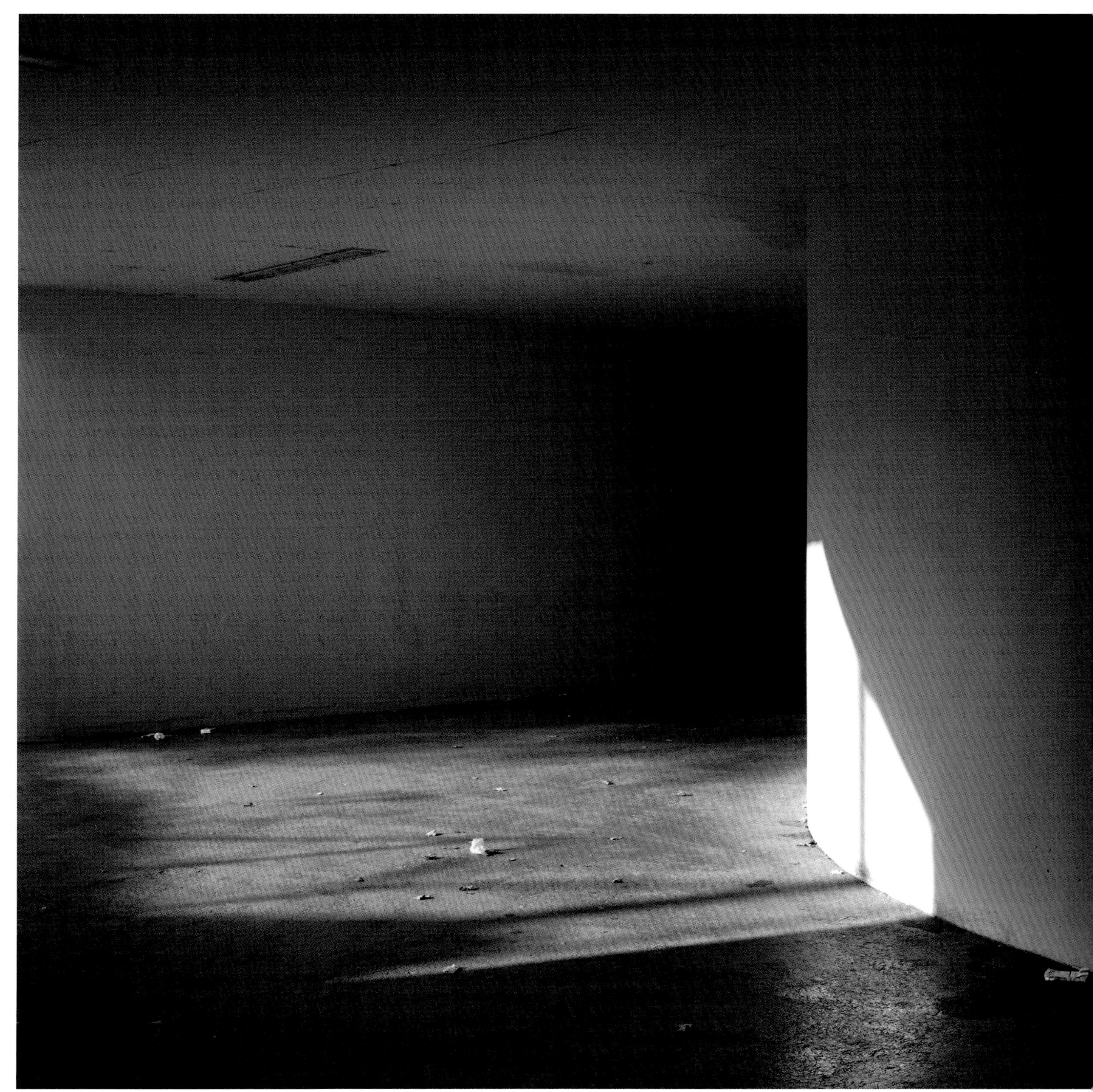

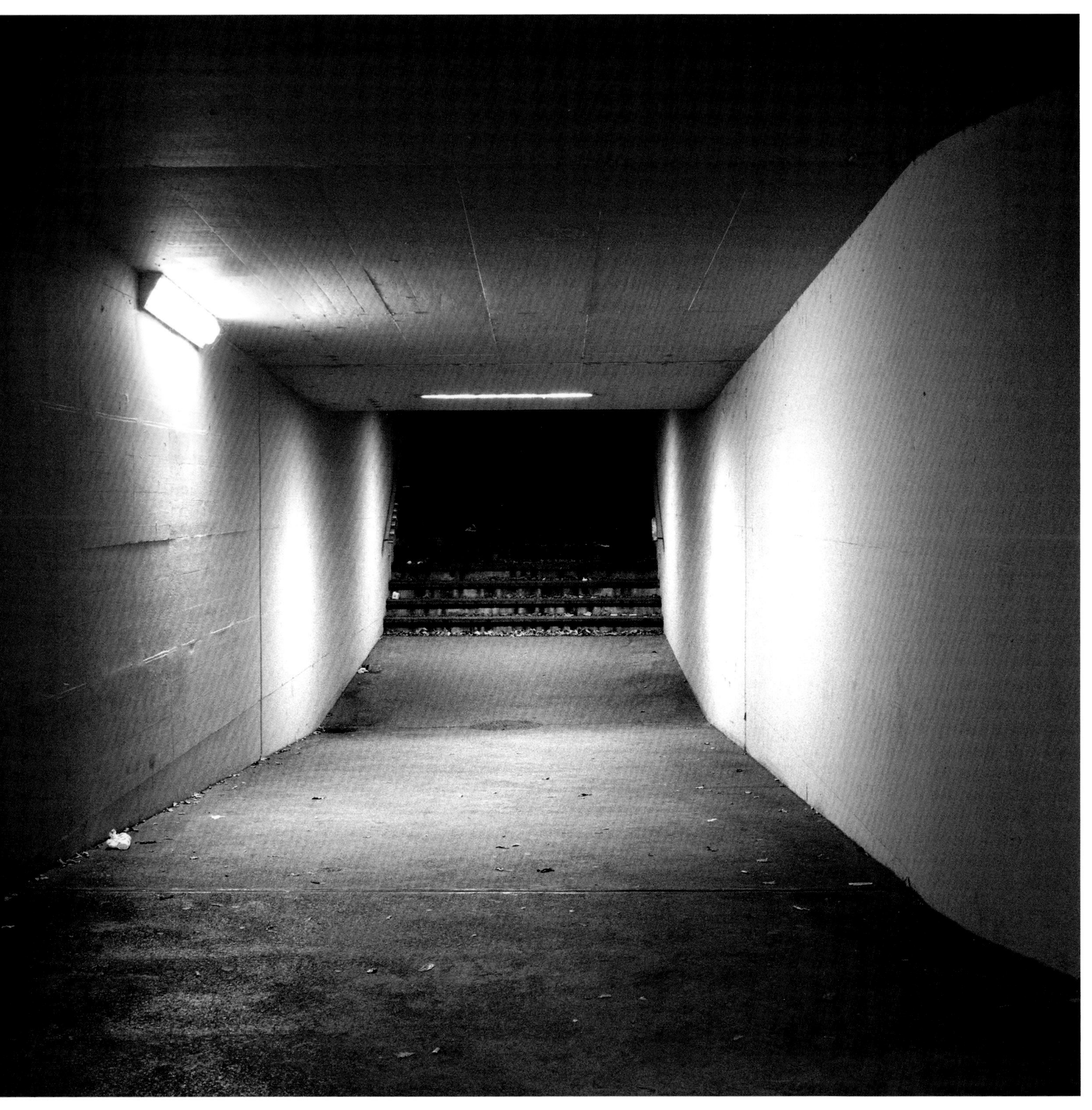

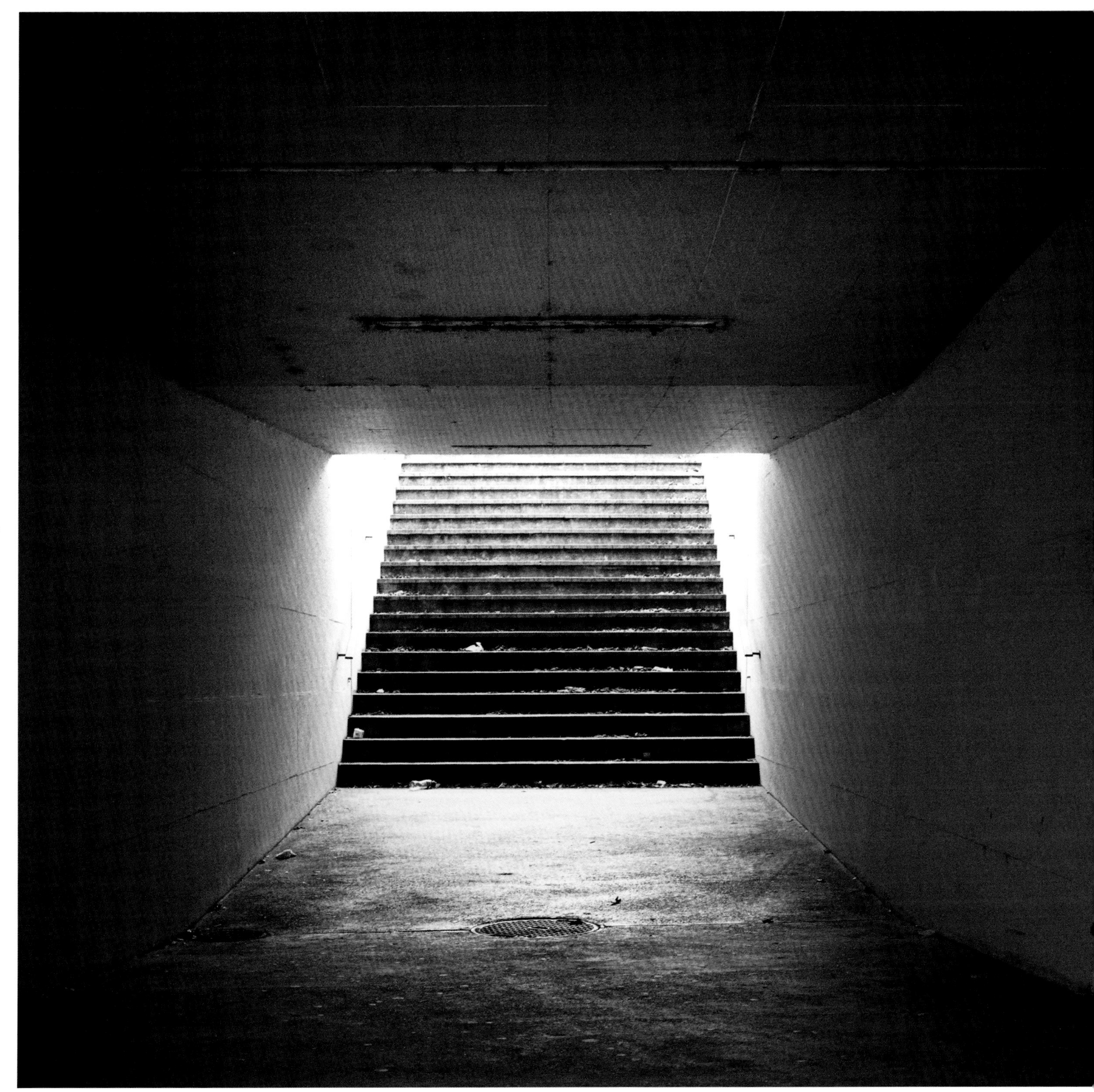

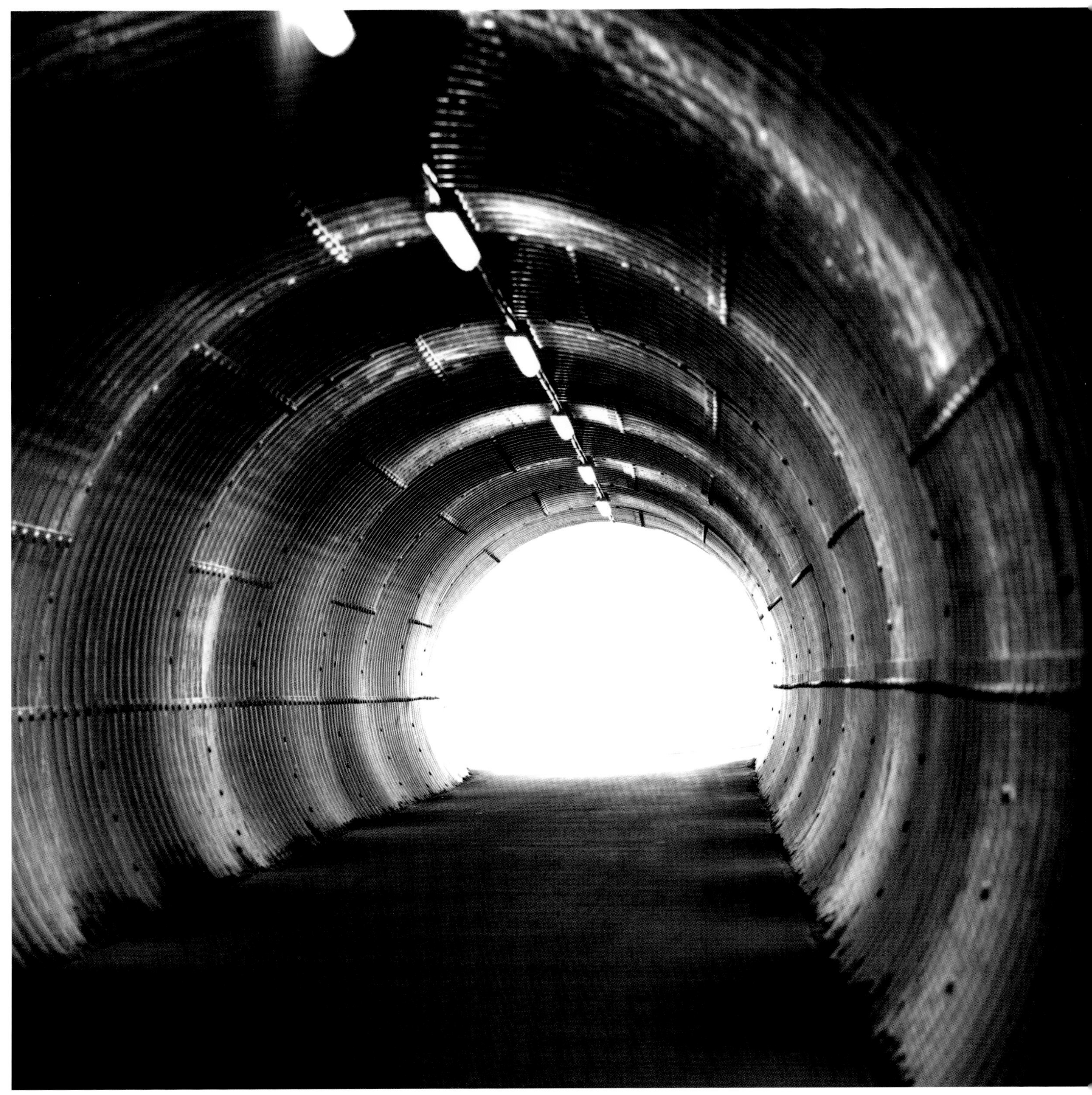

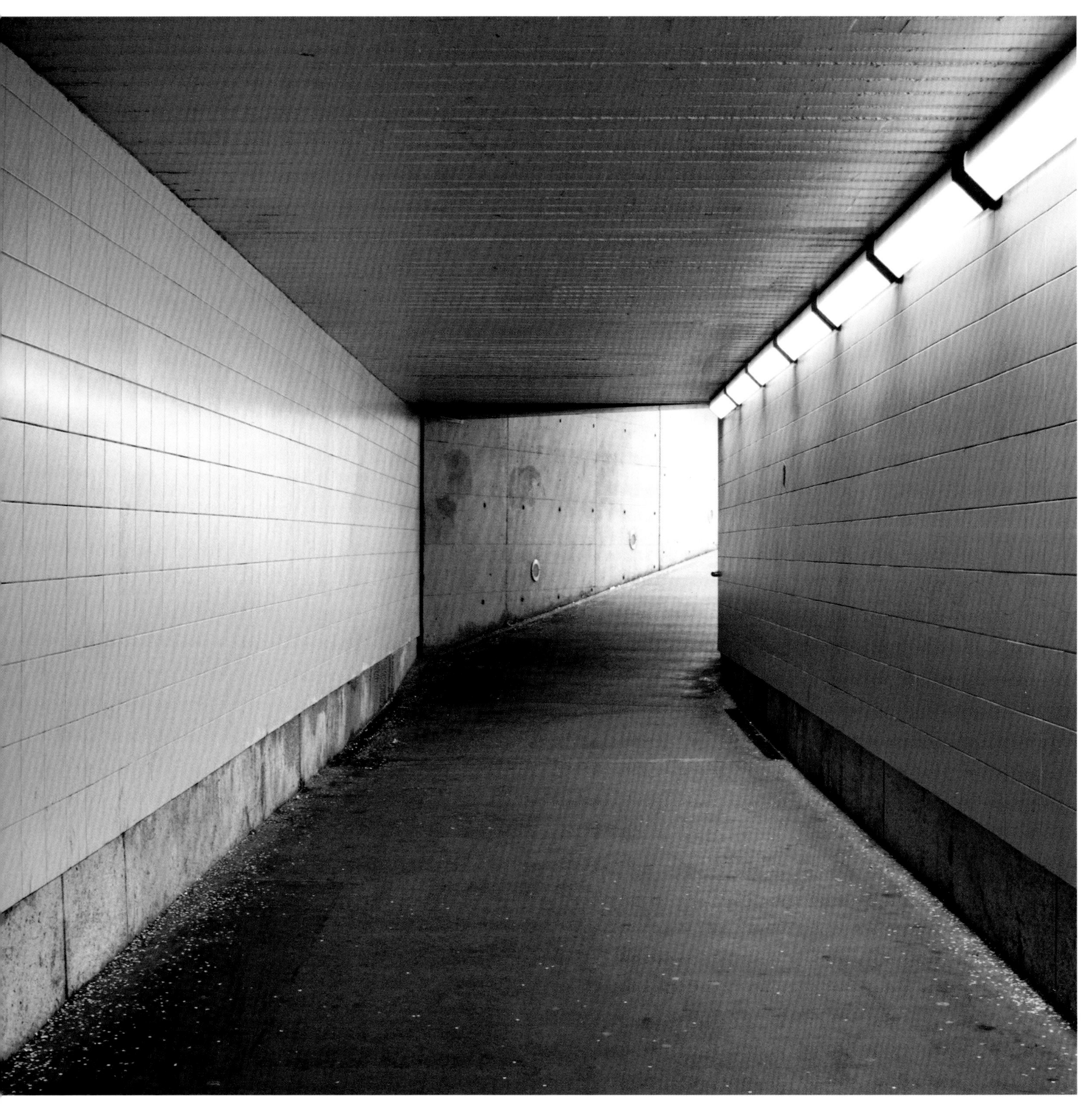

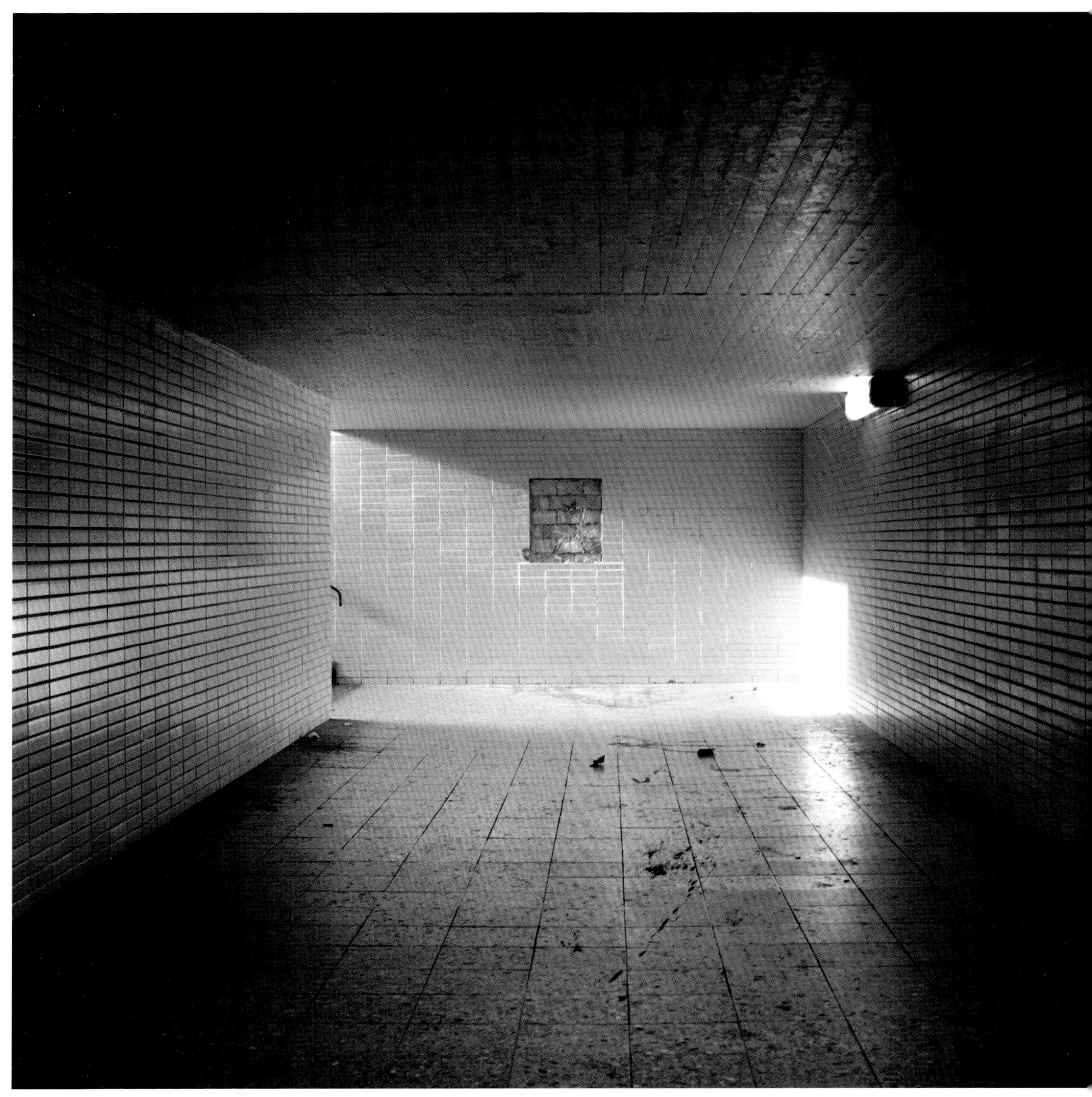

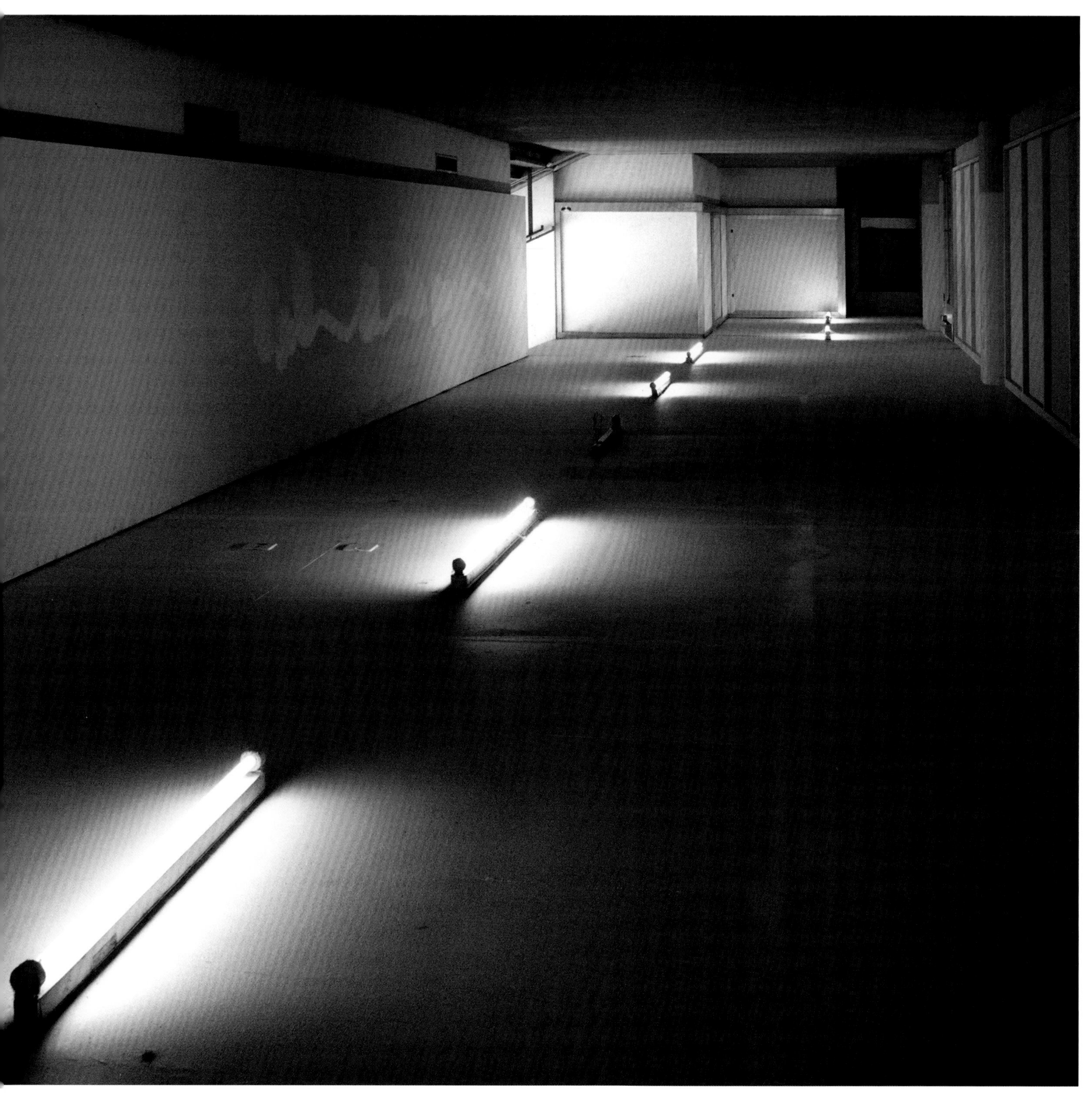

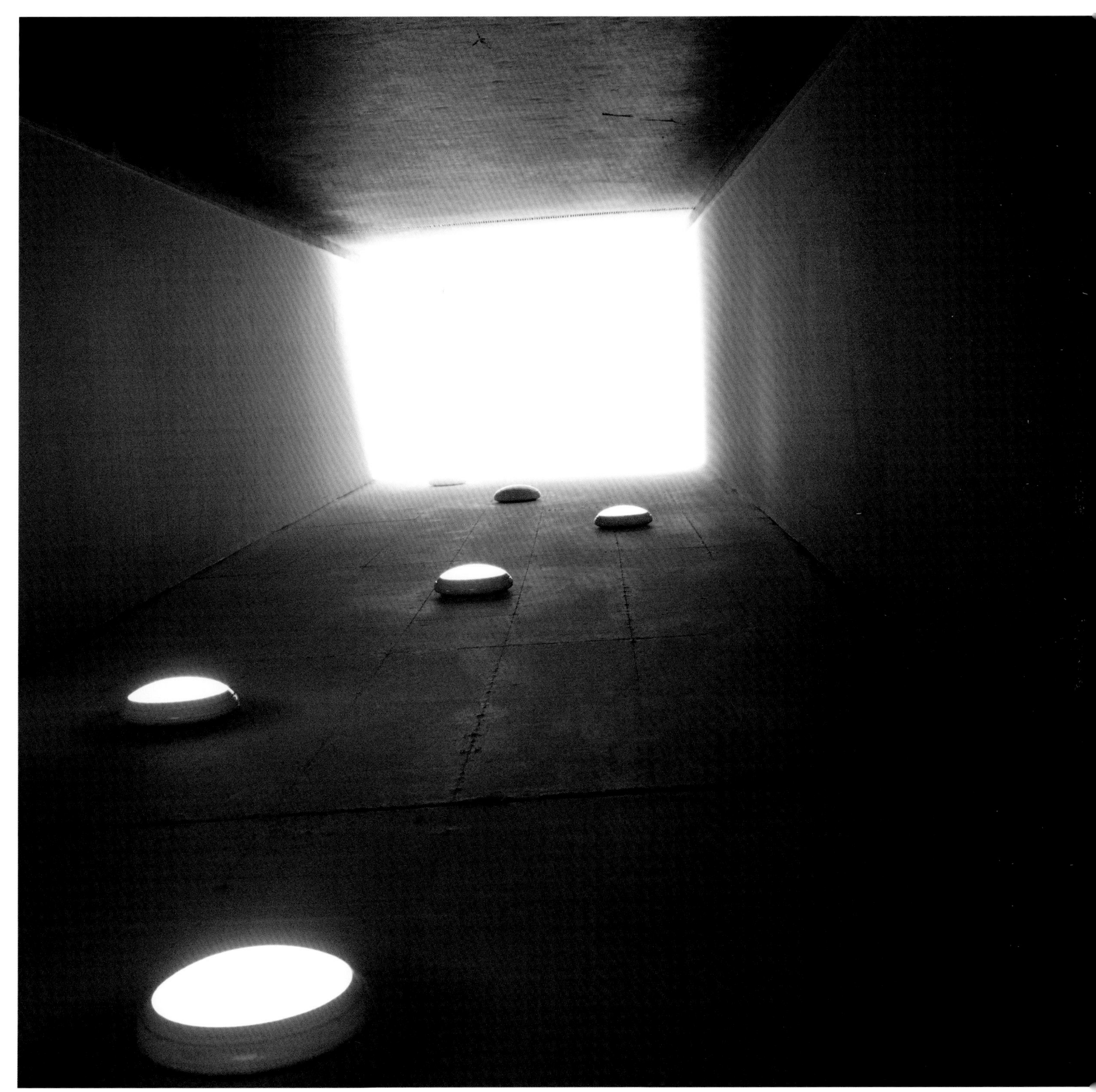

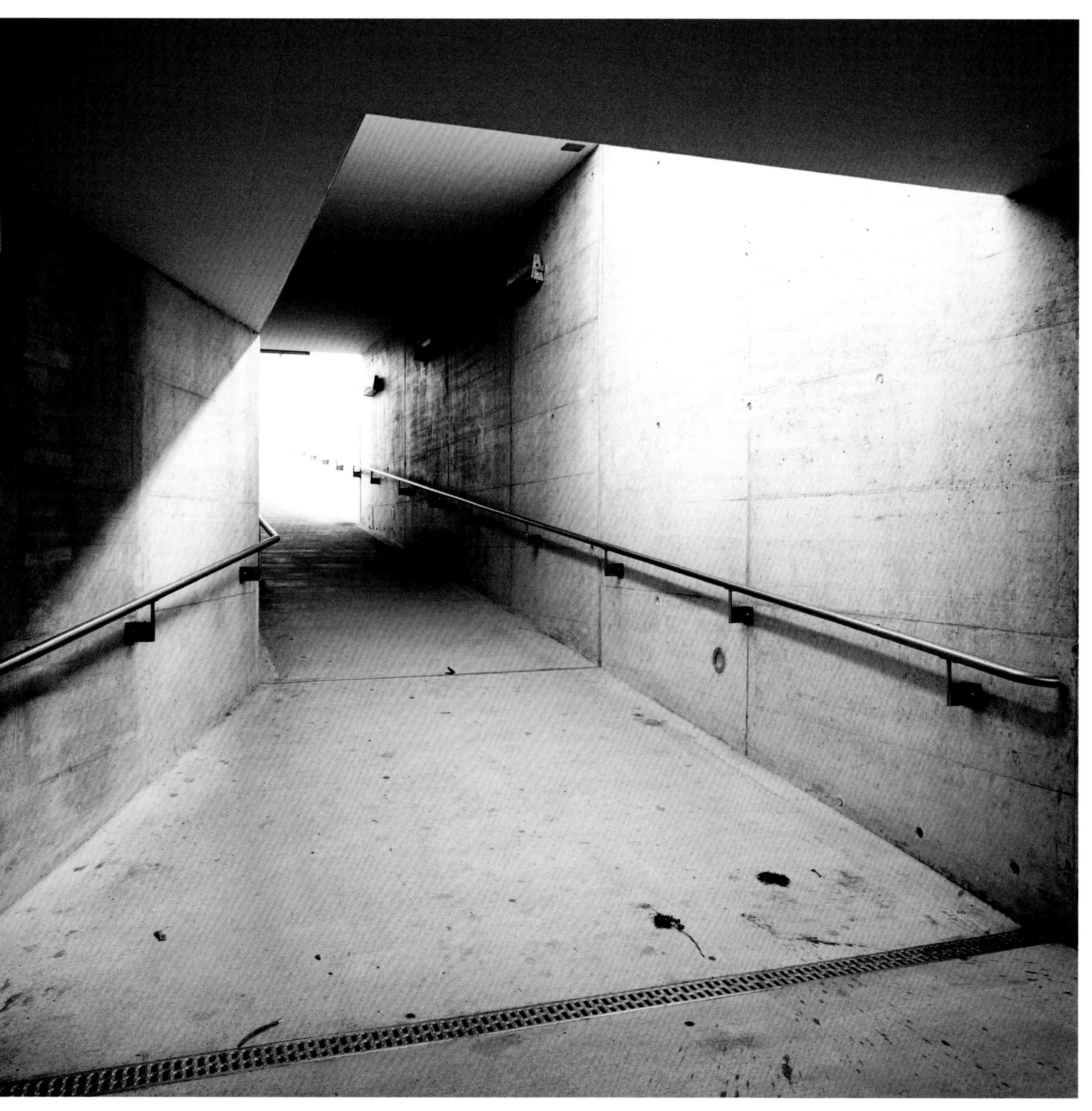

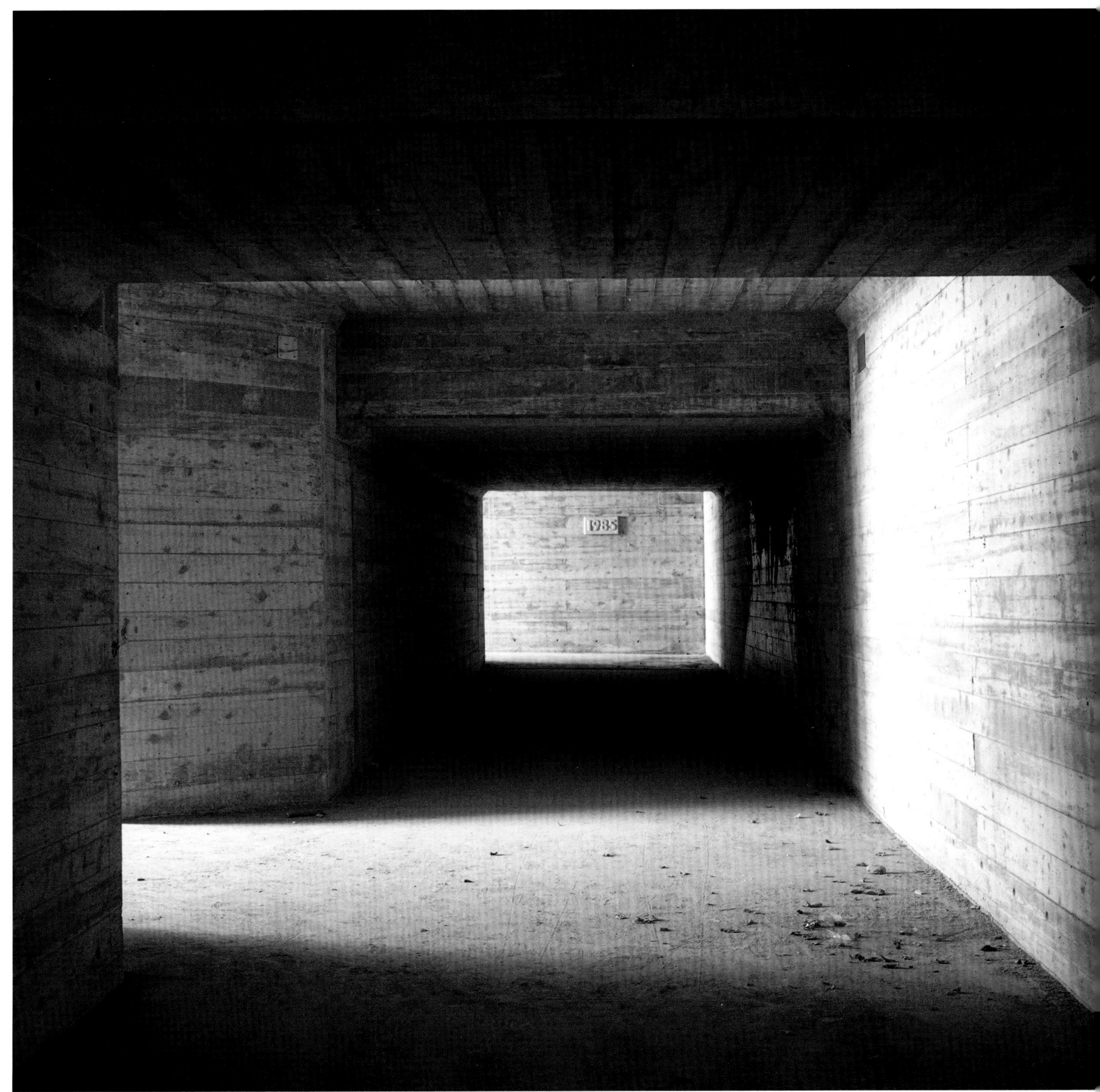
1985

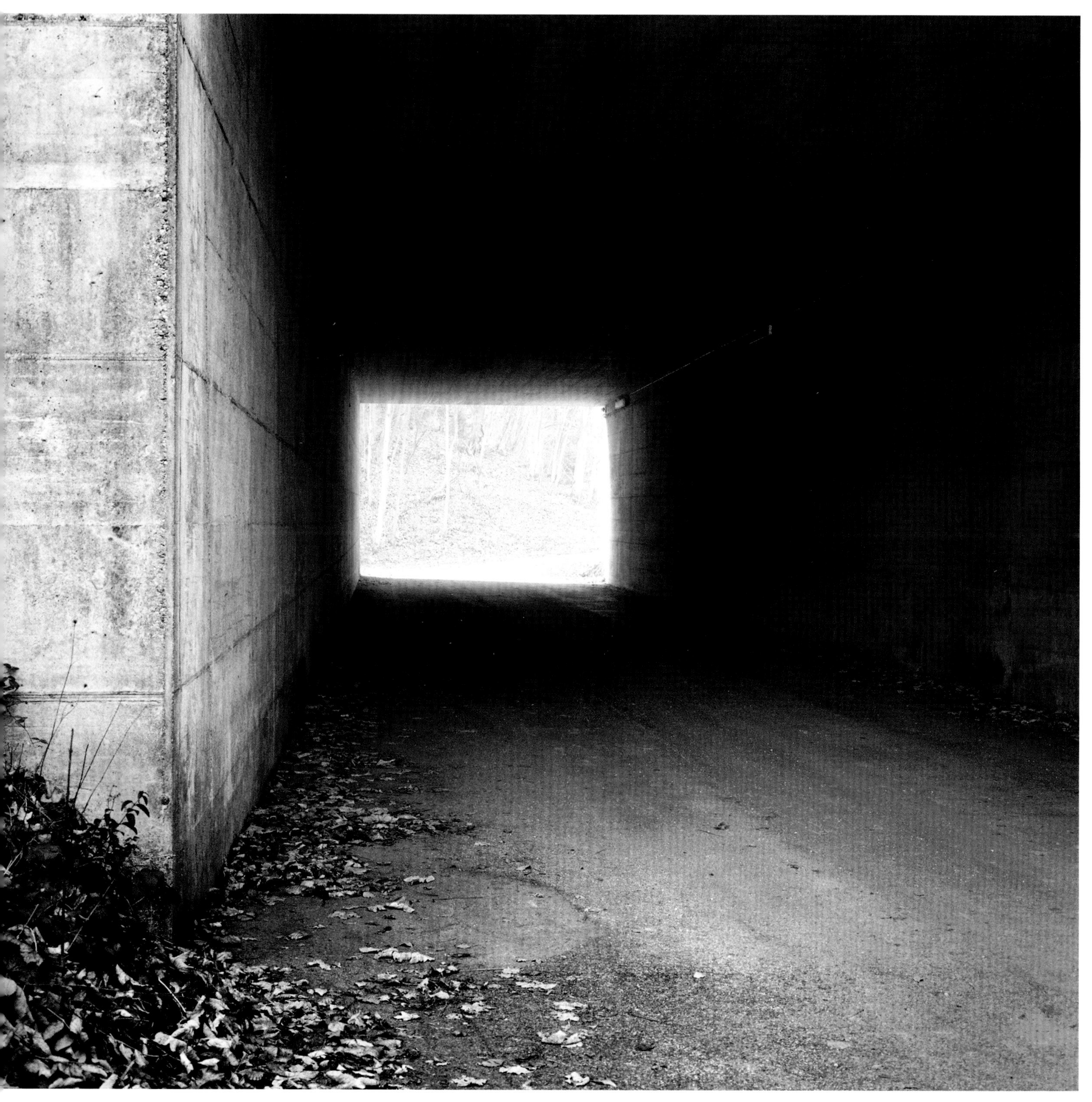

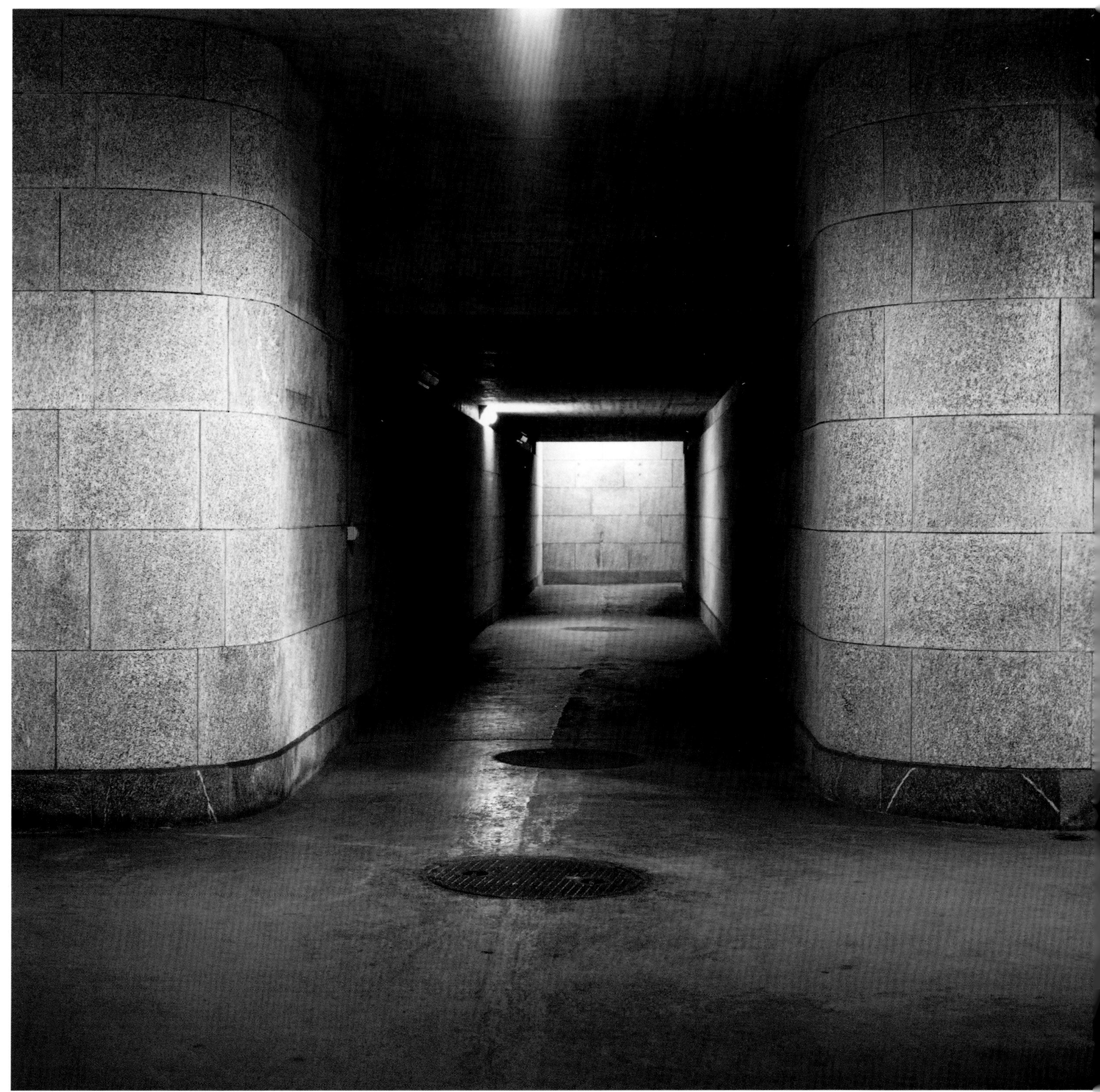

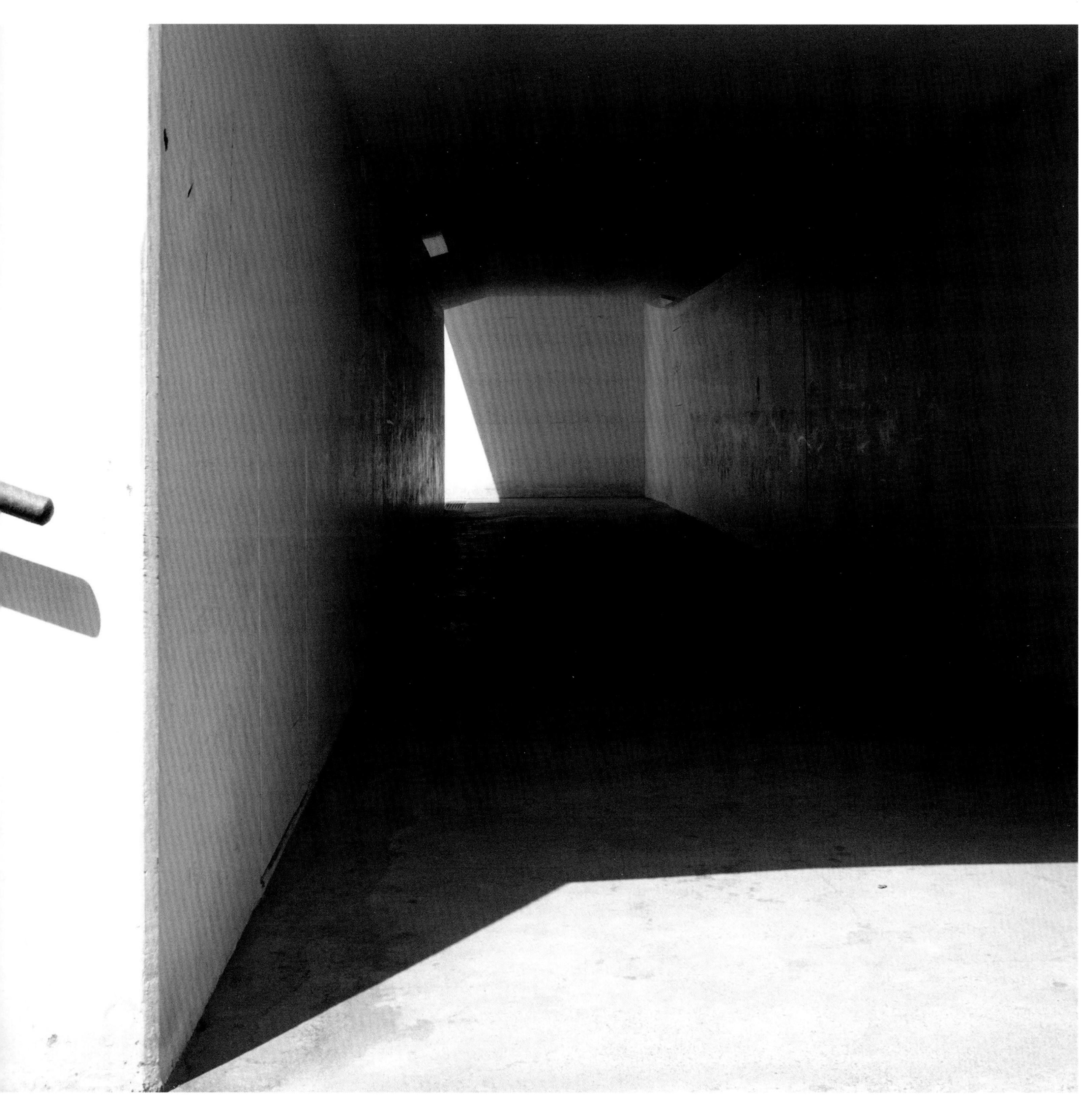

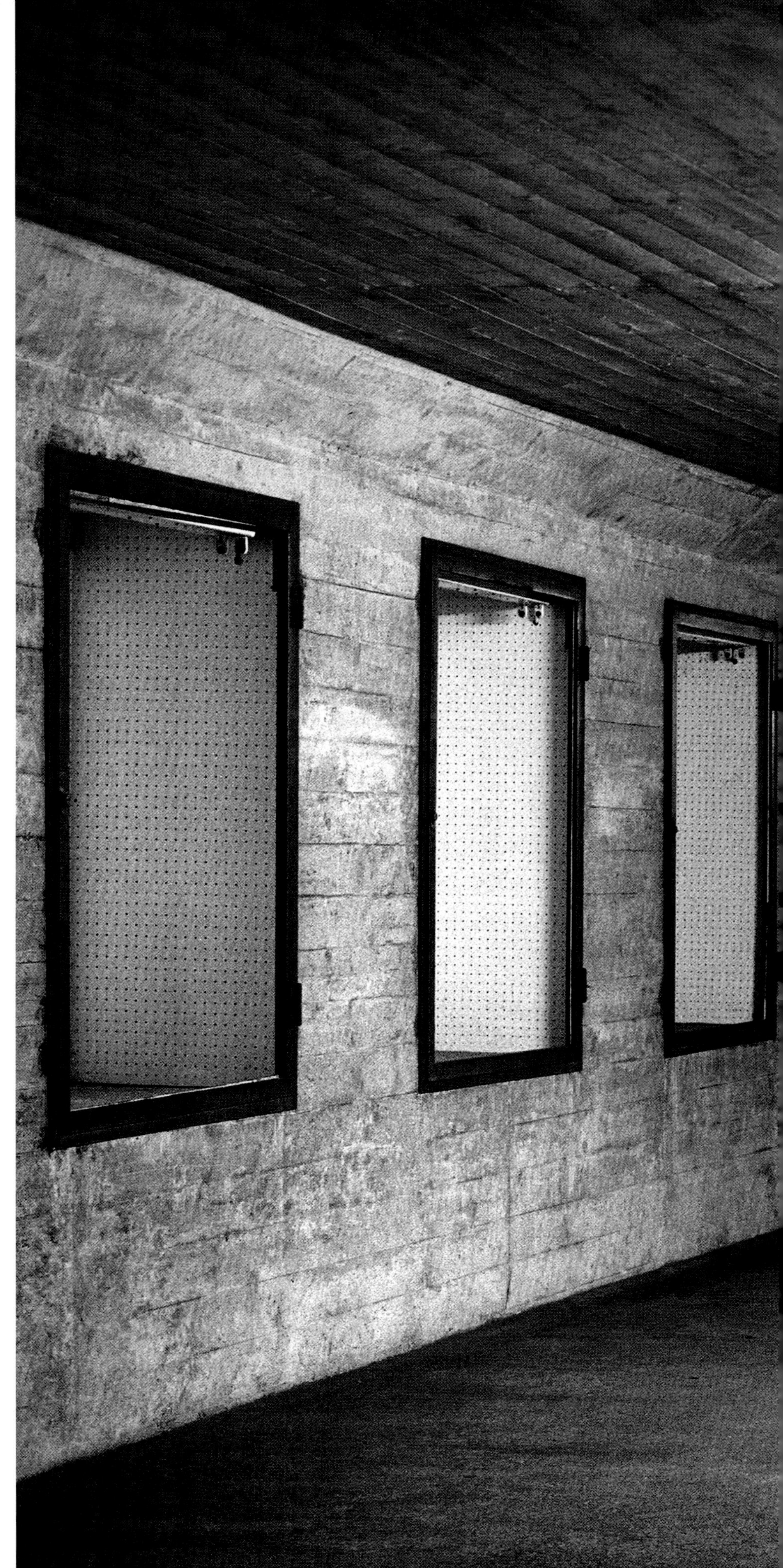

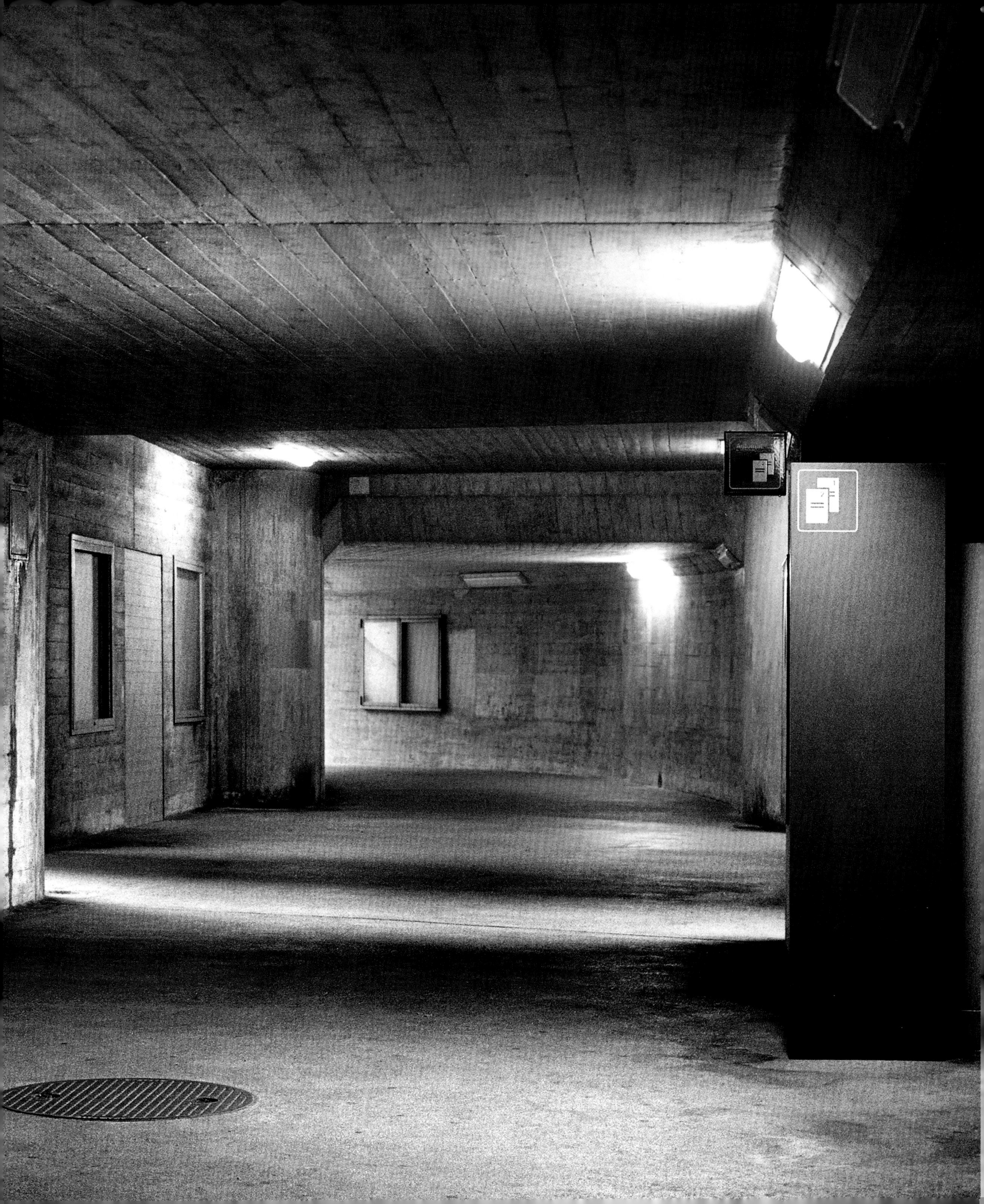

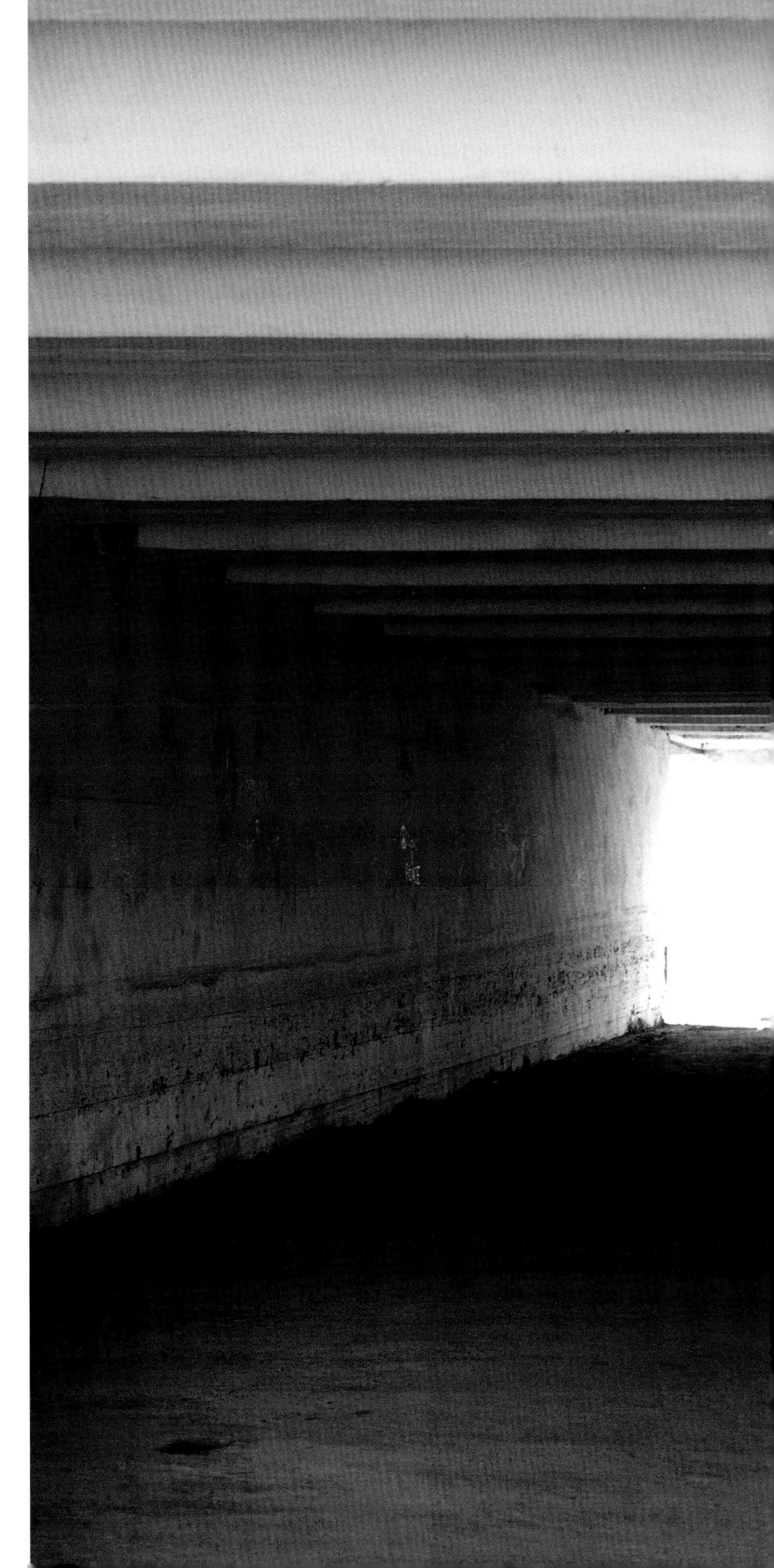

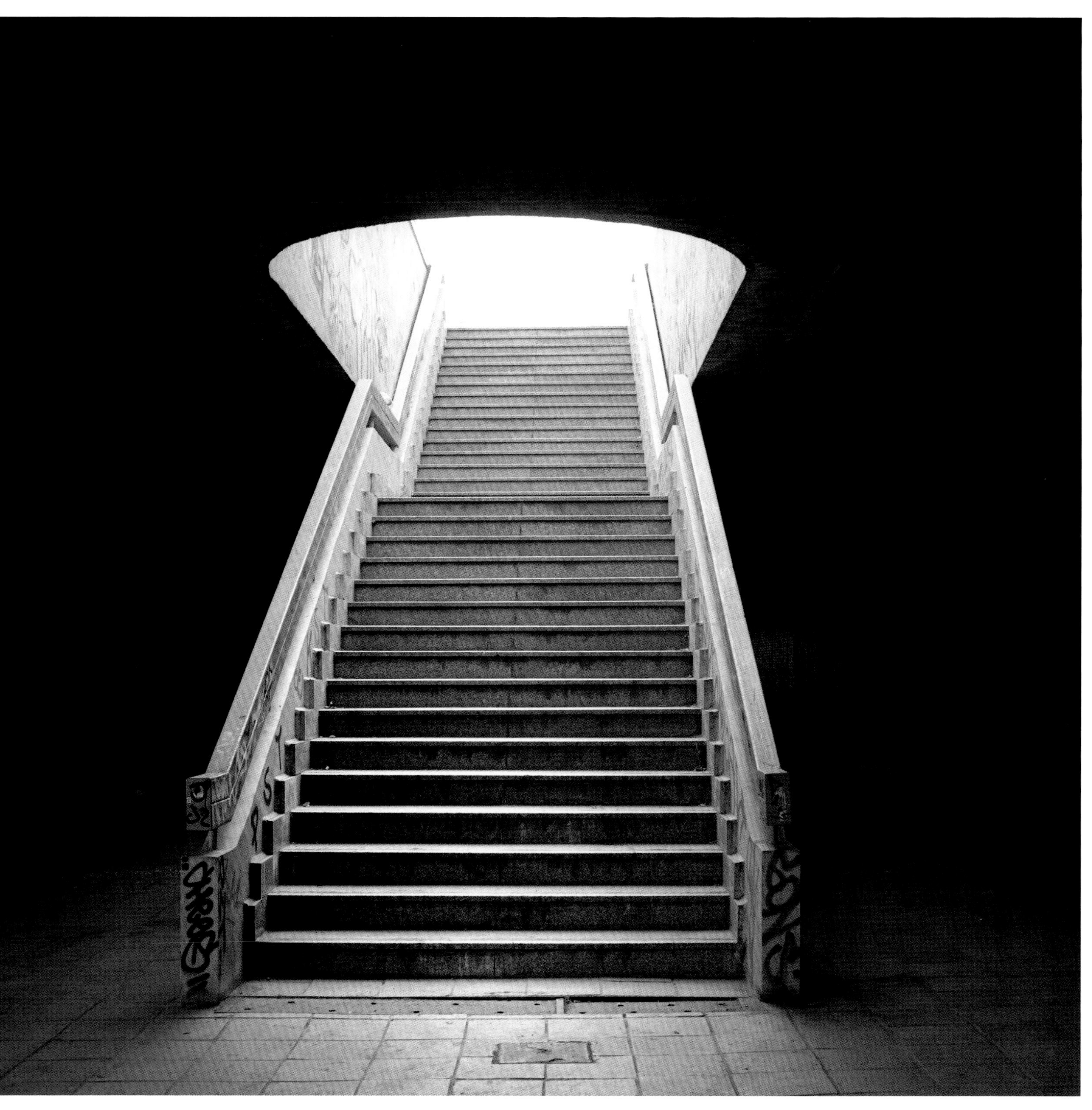

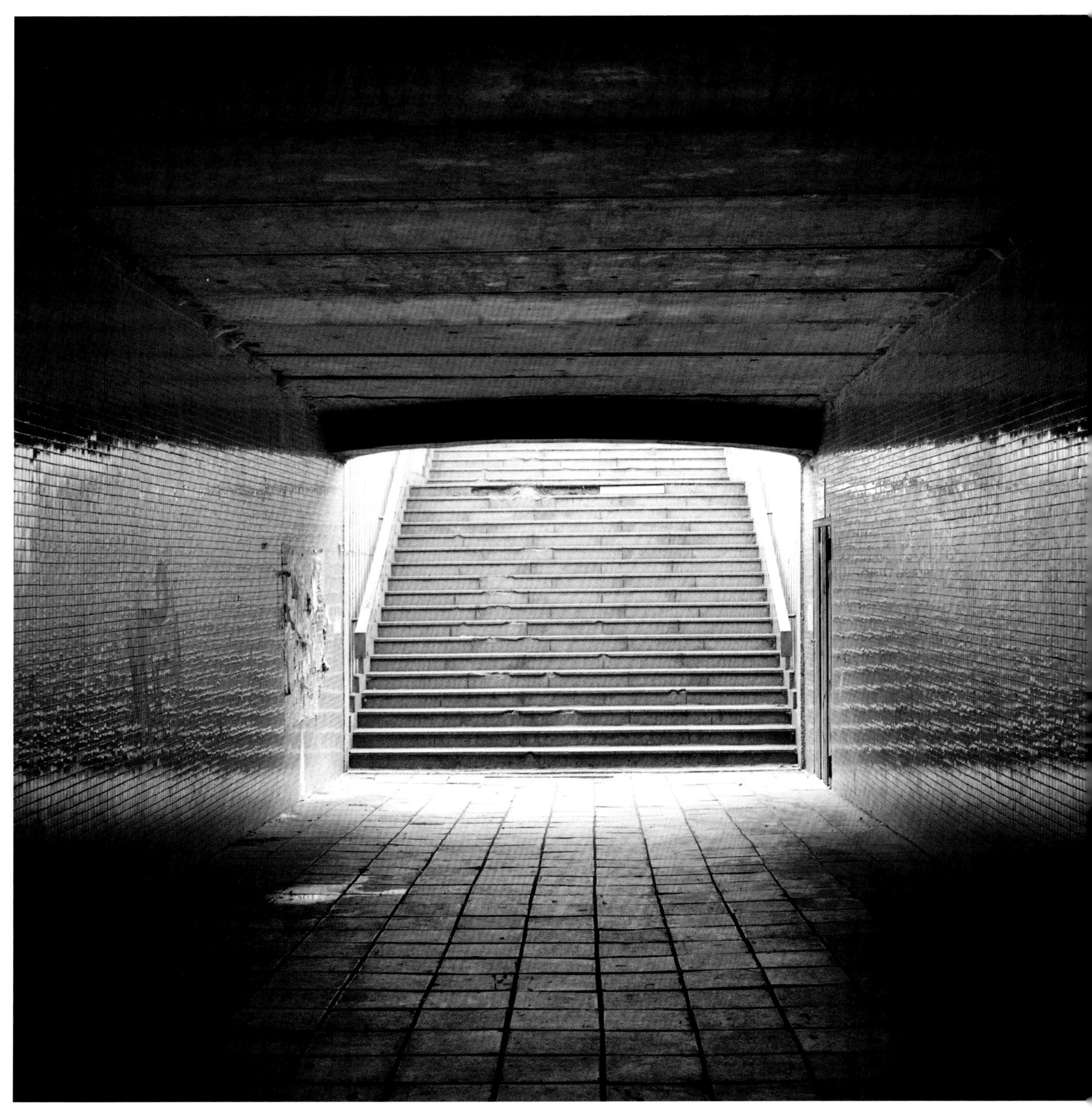

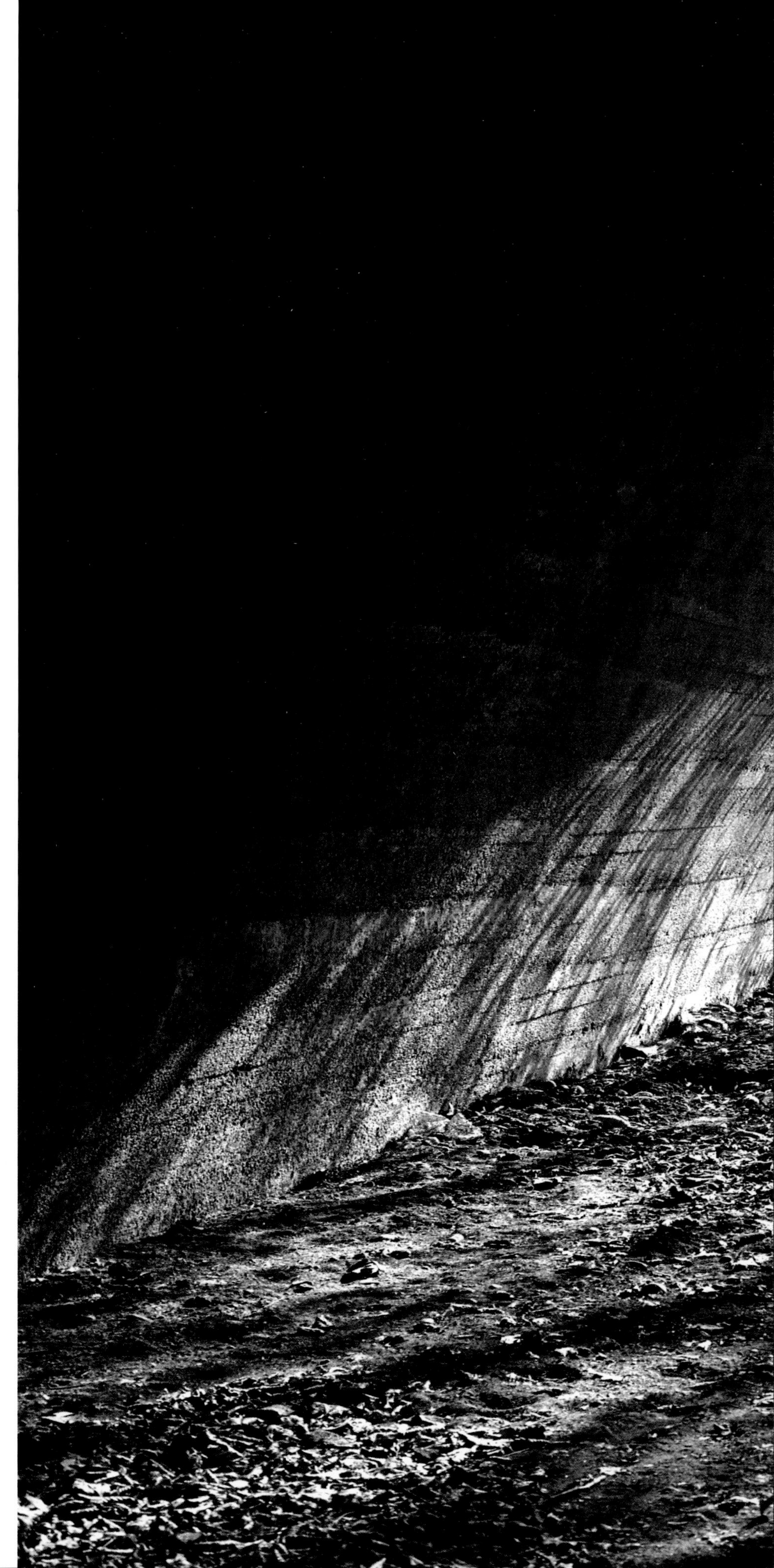

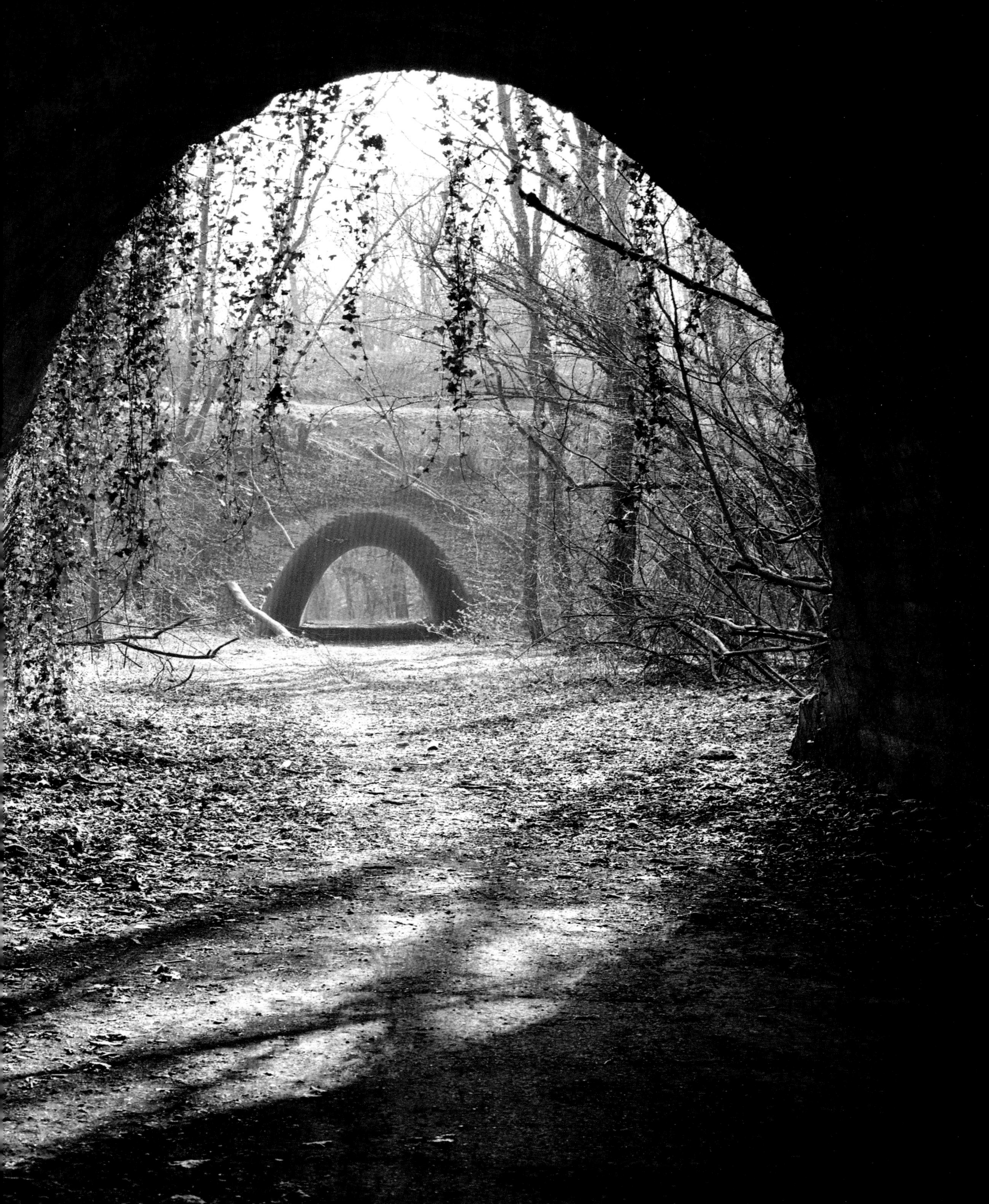

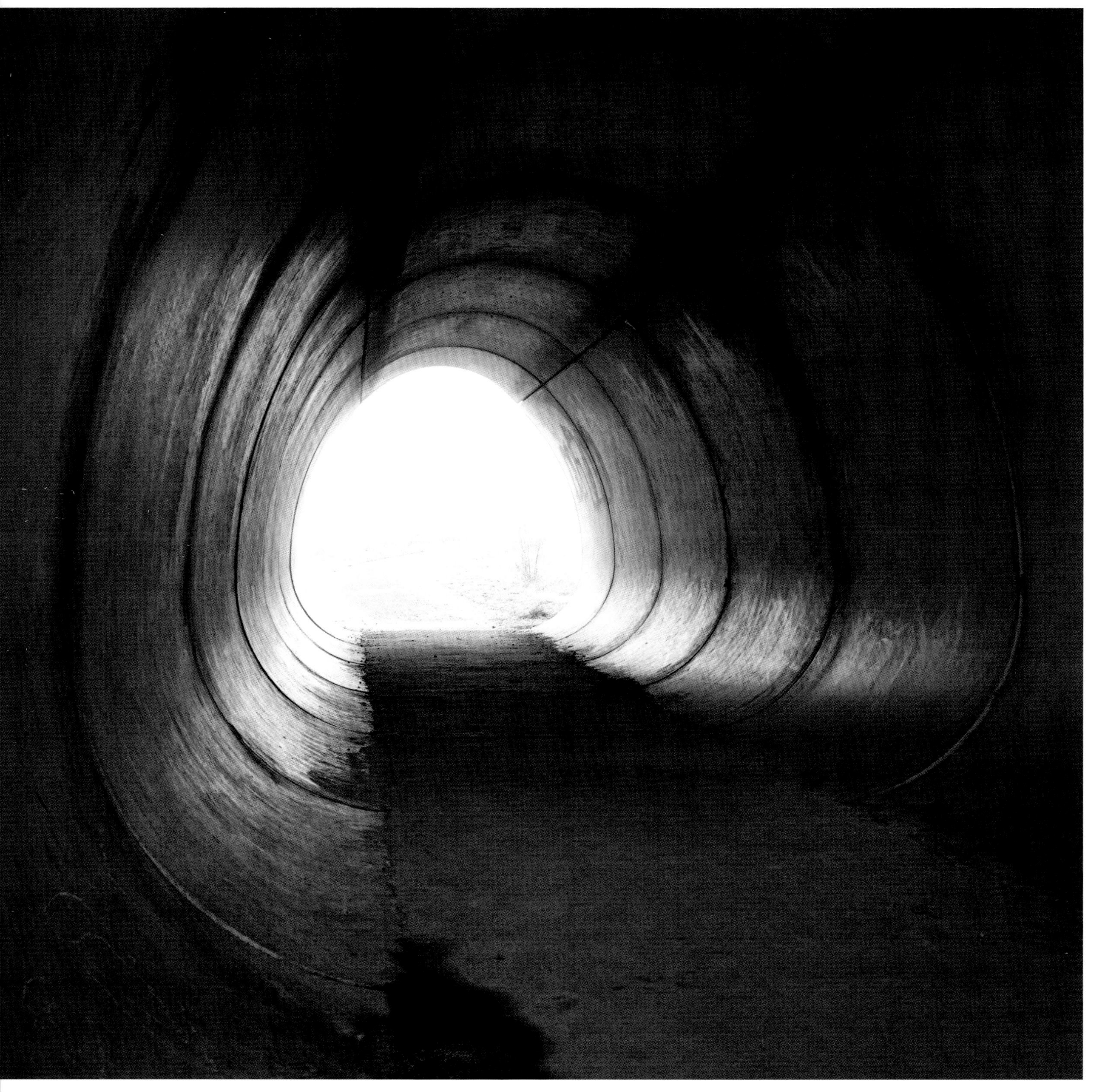

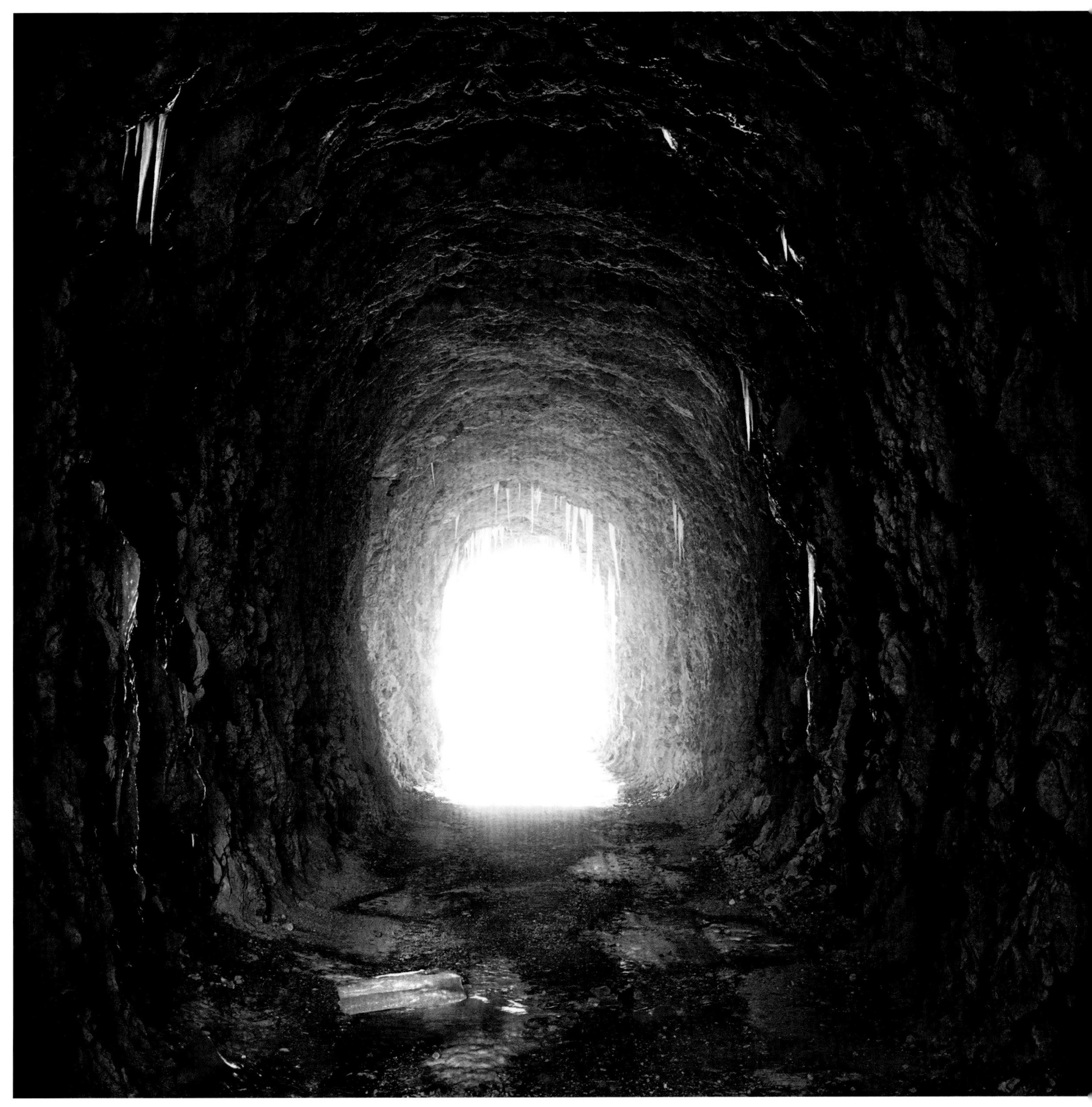

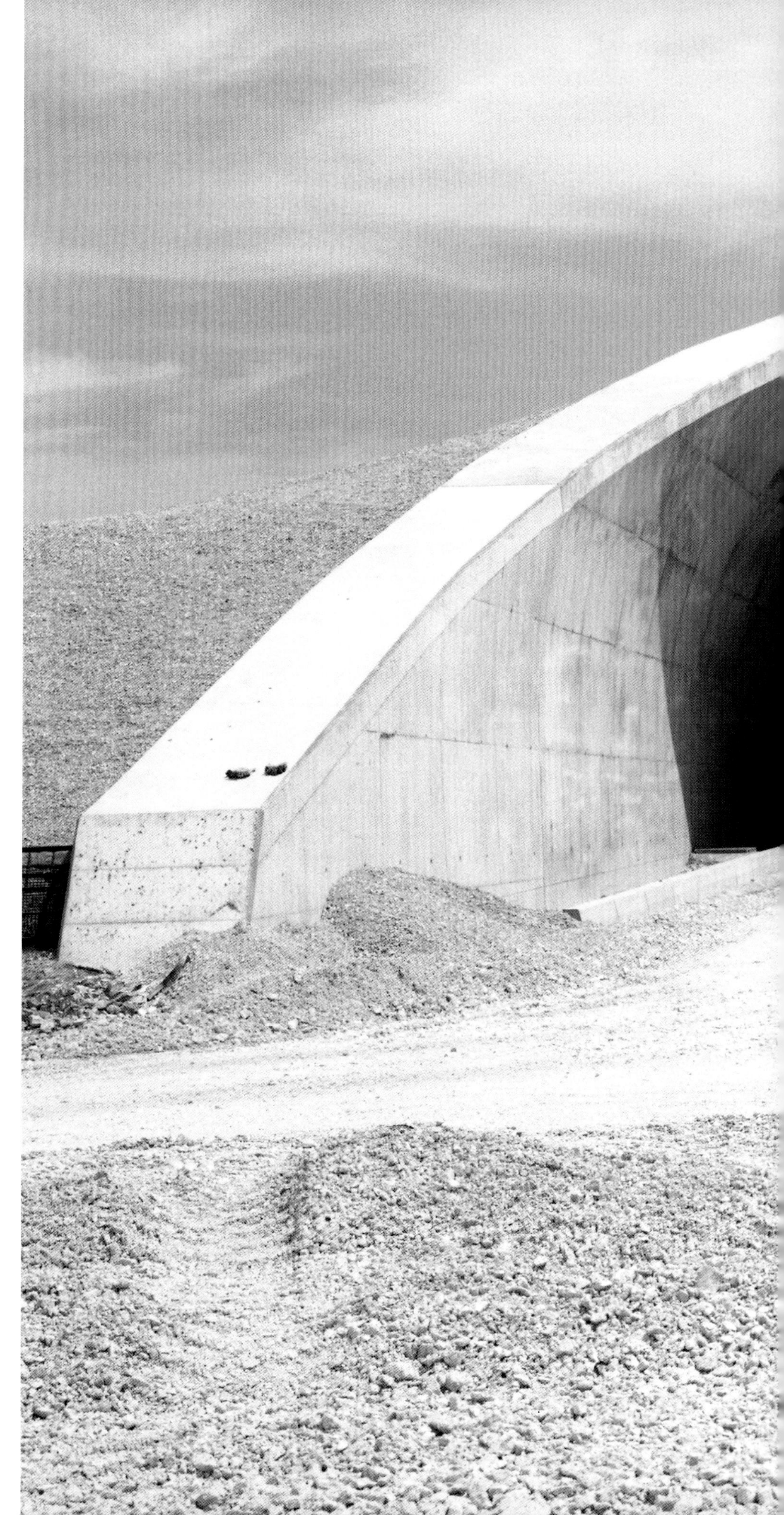

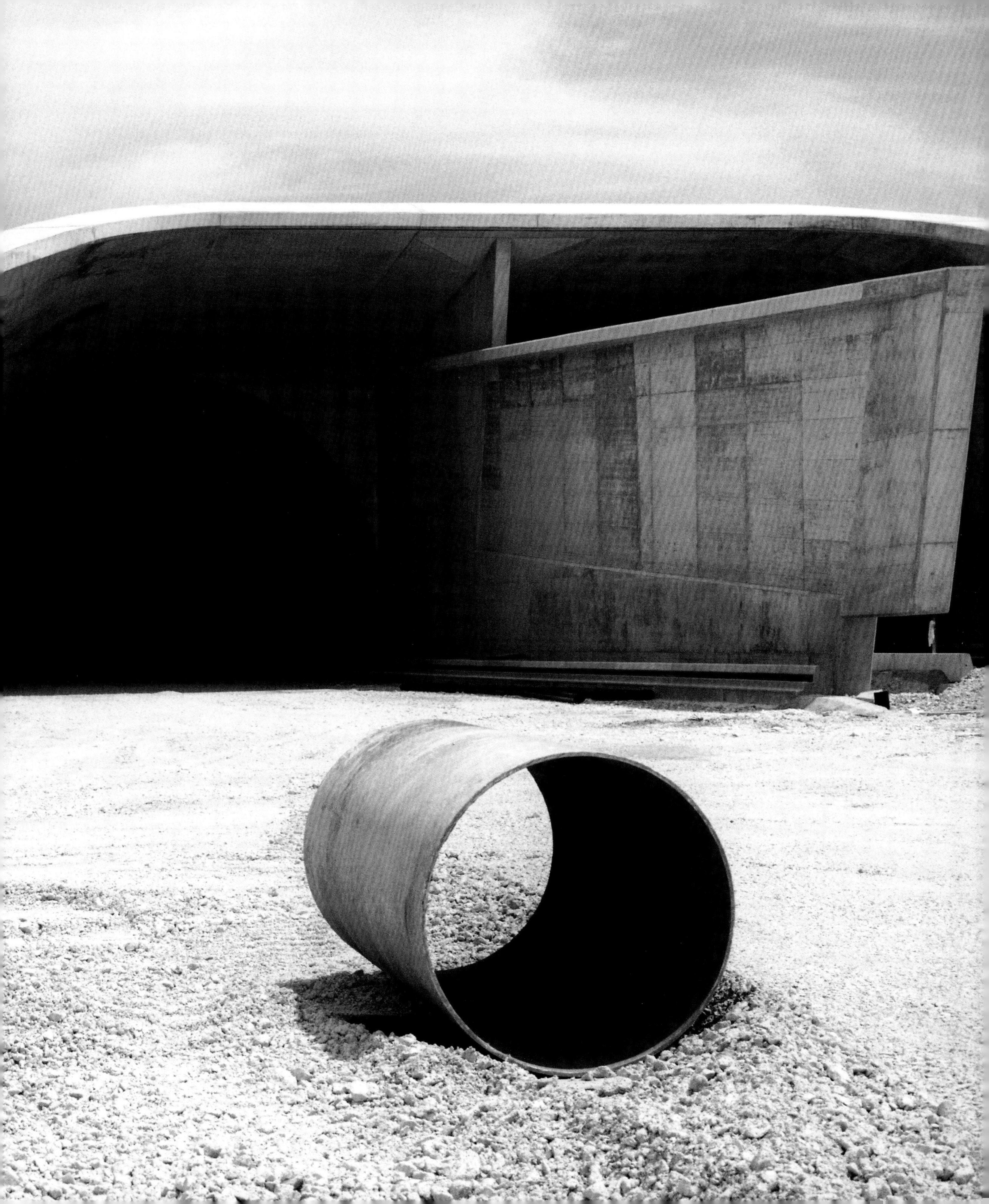

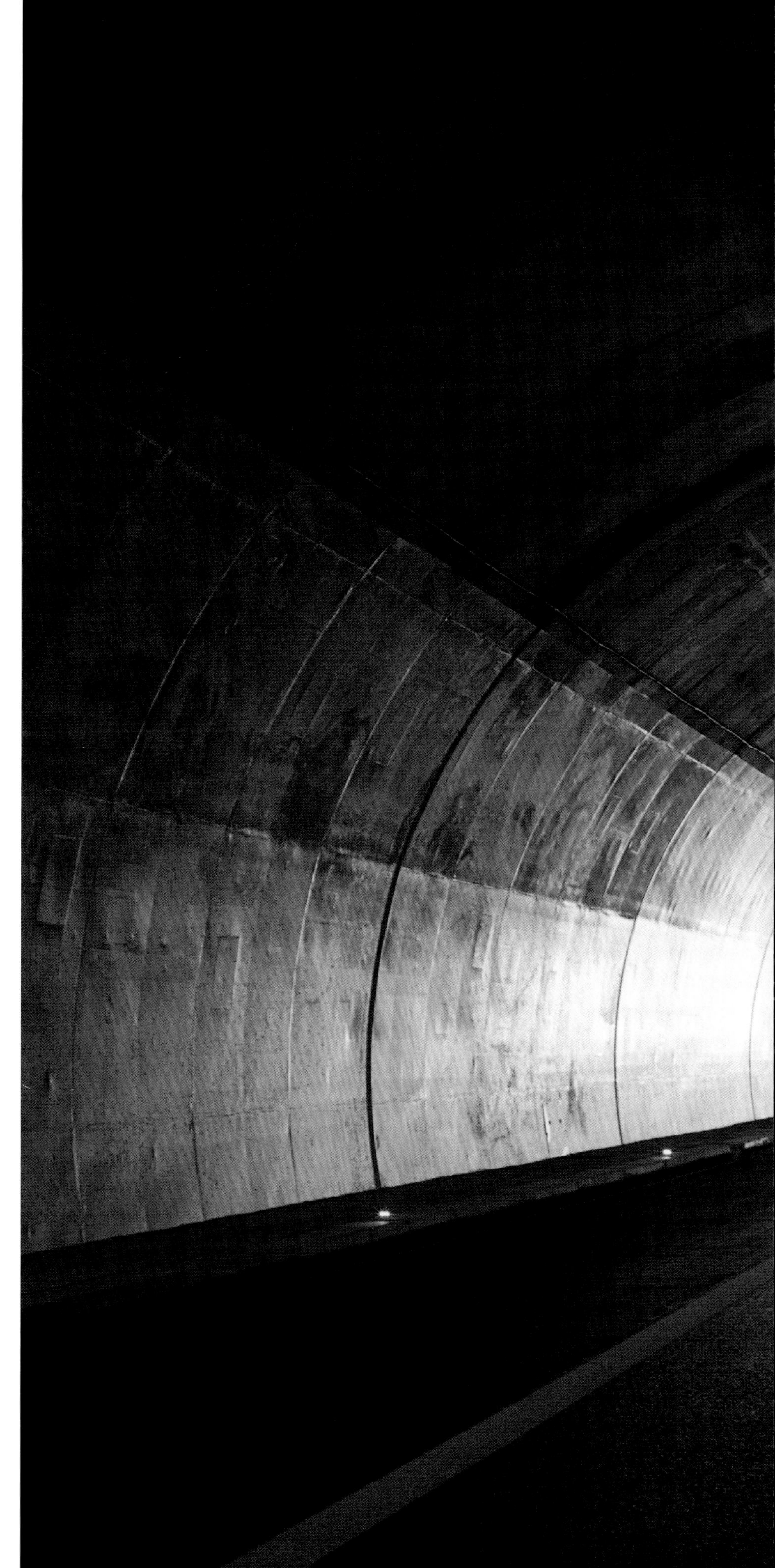

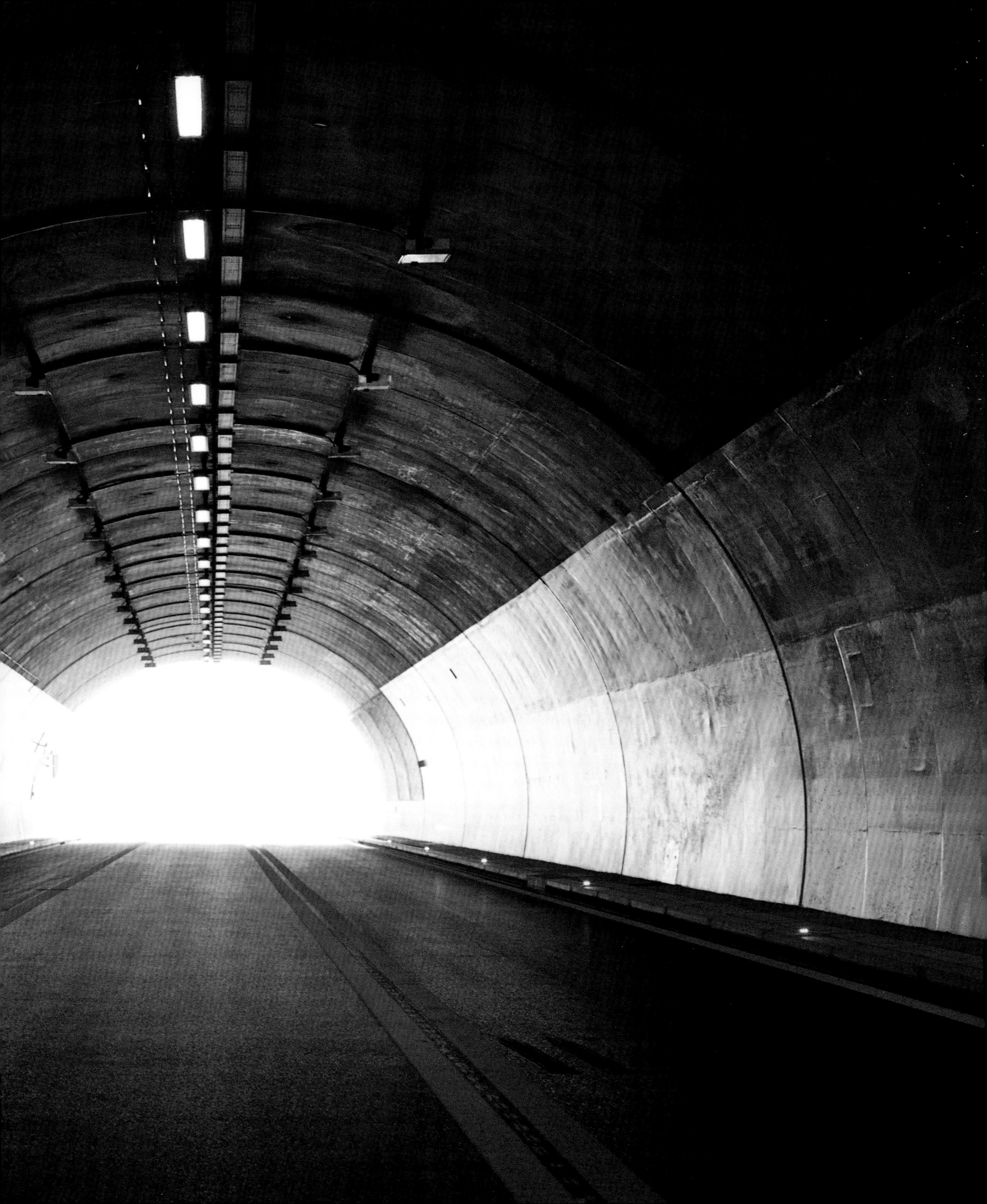

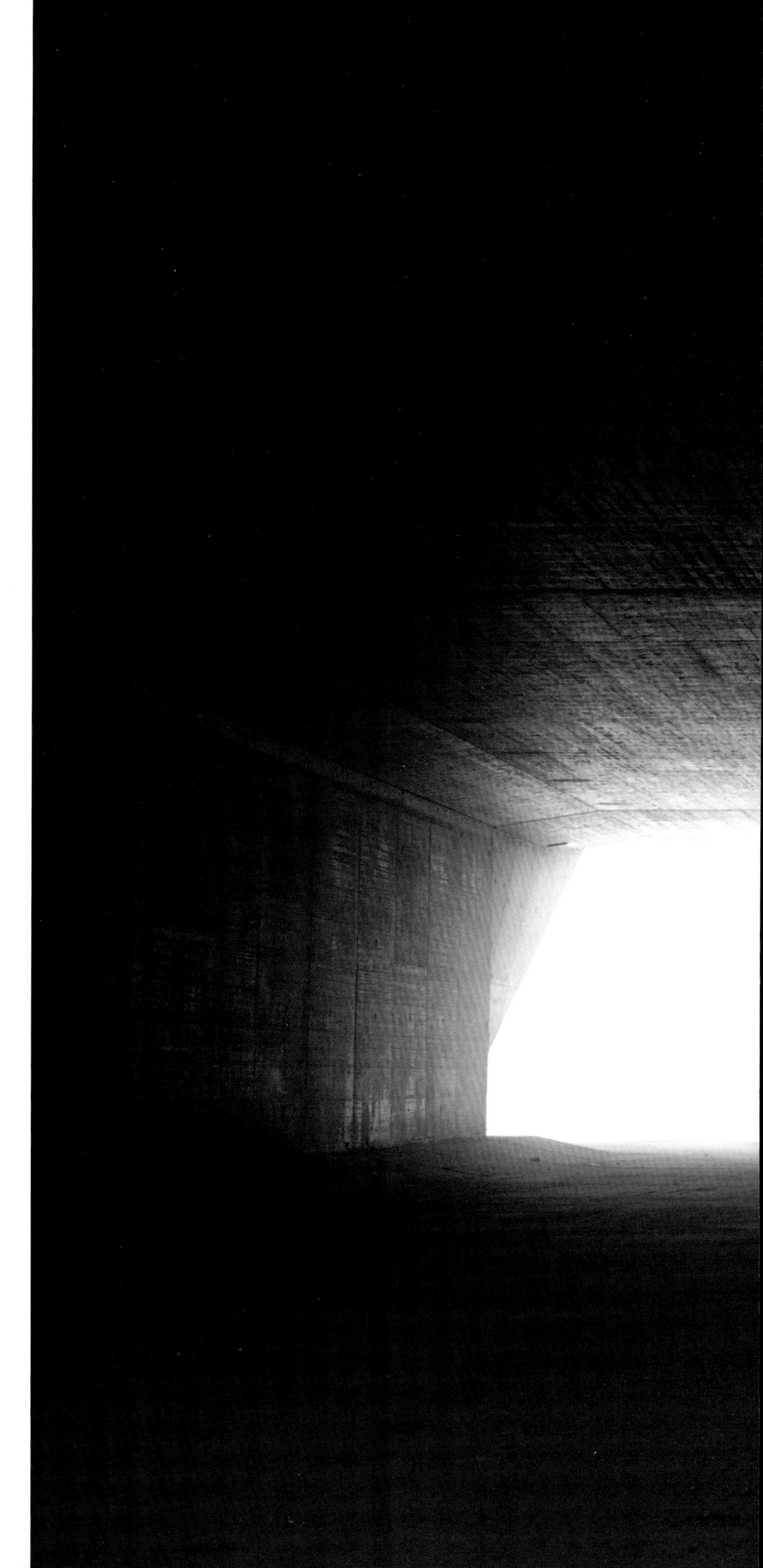

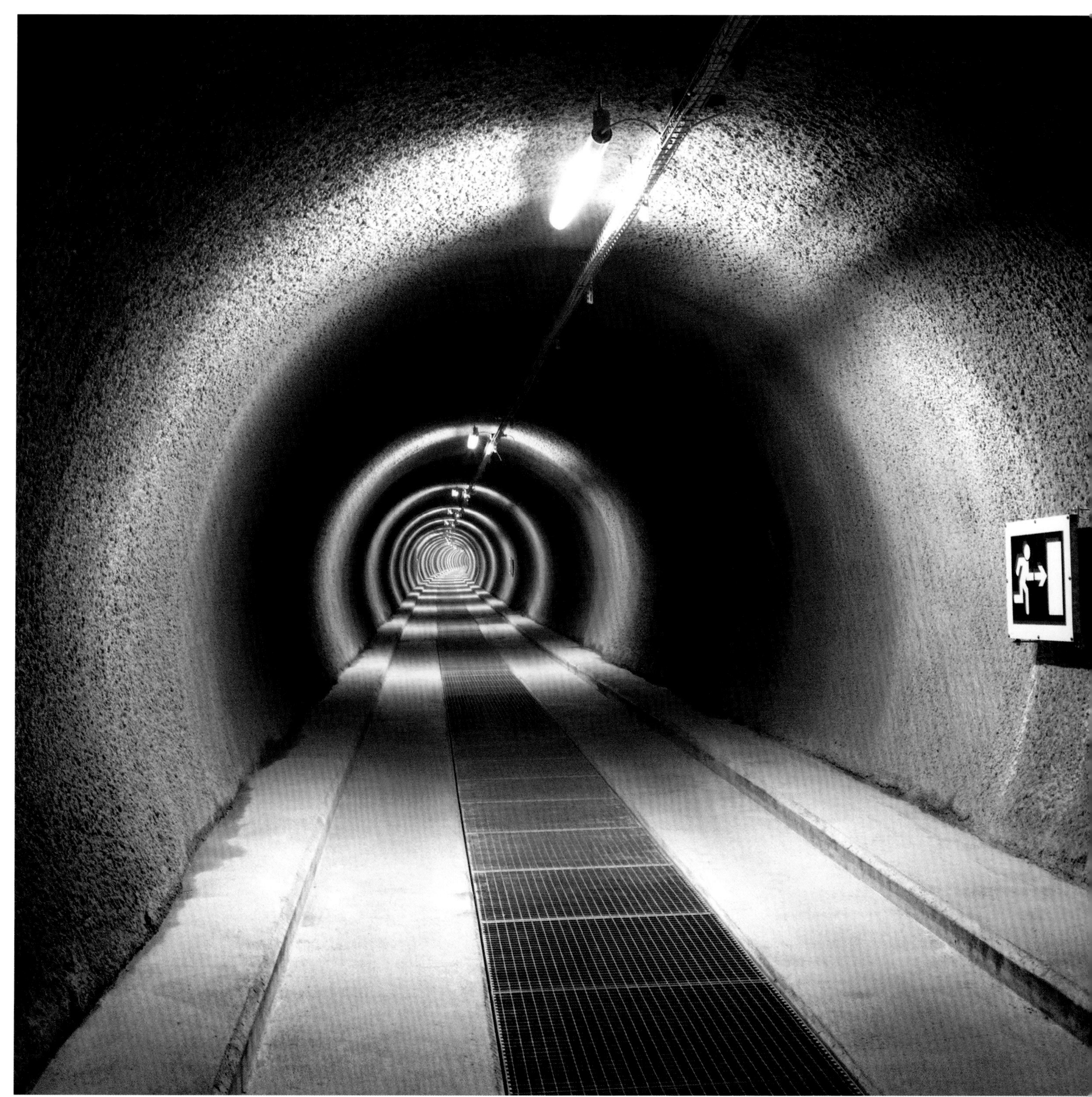

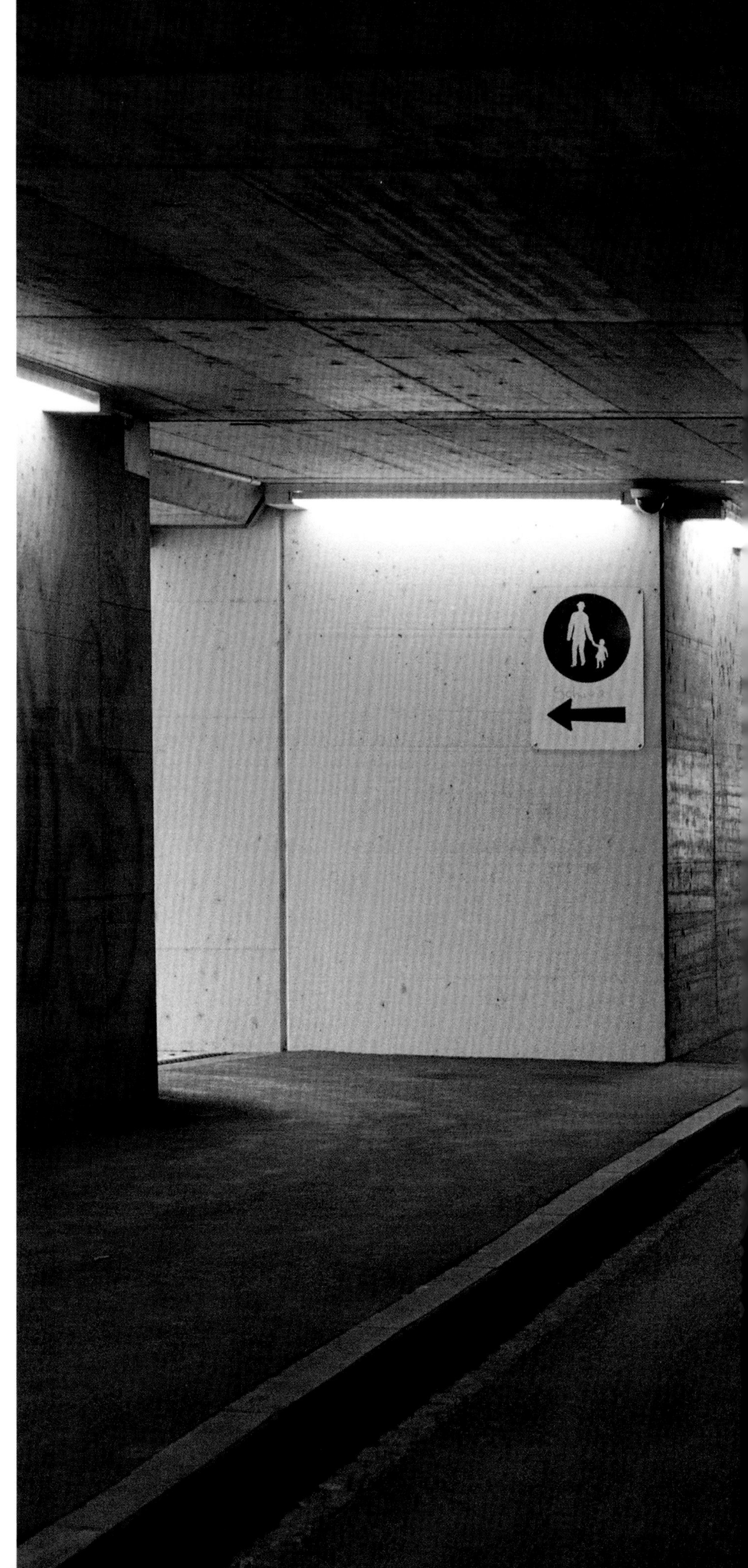

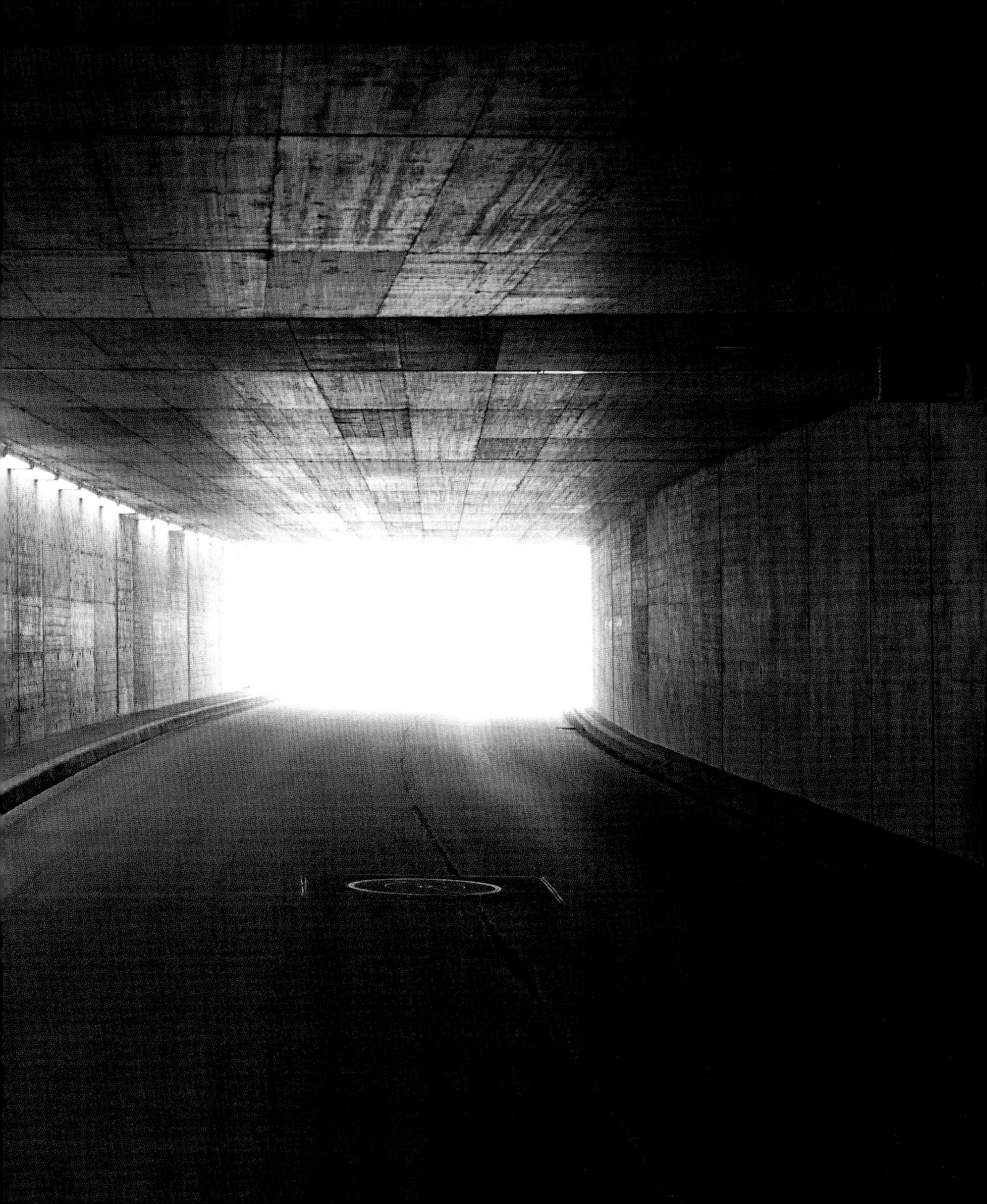

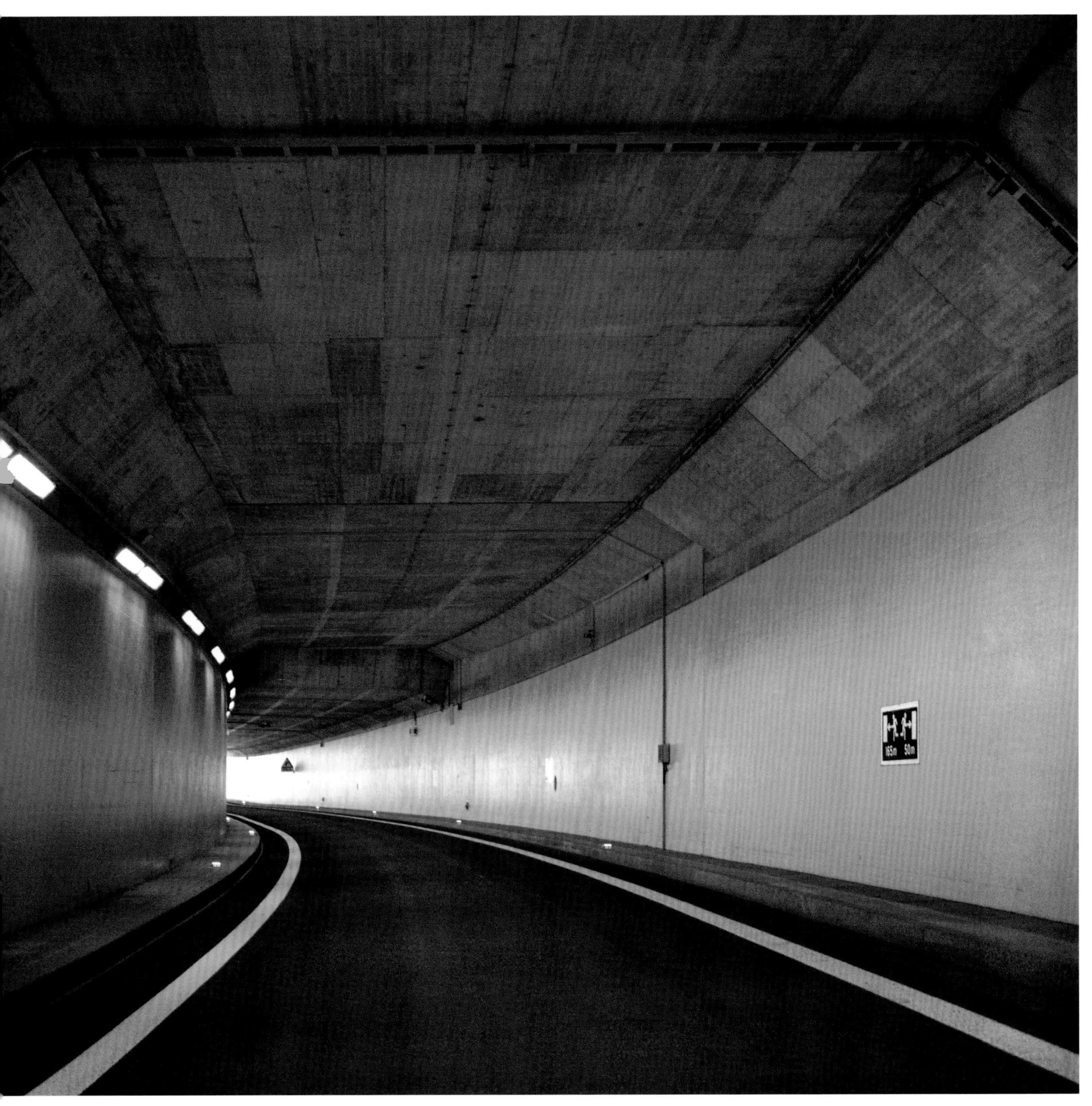
165m 50m

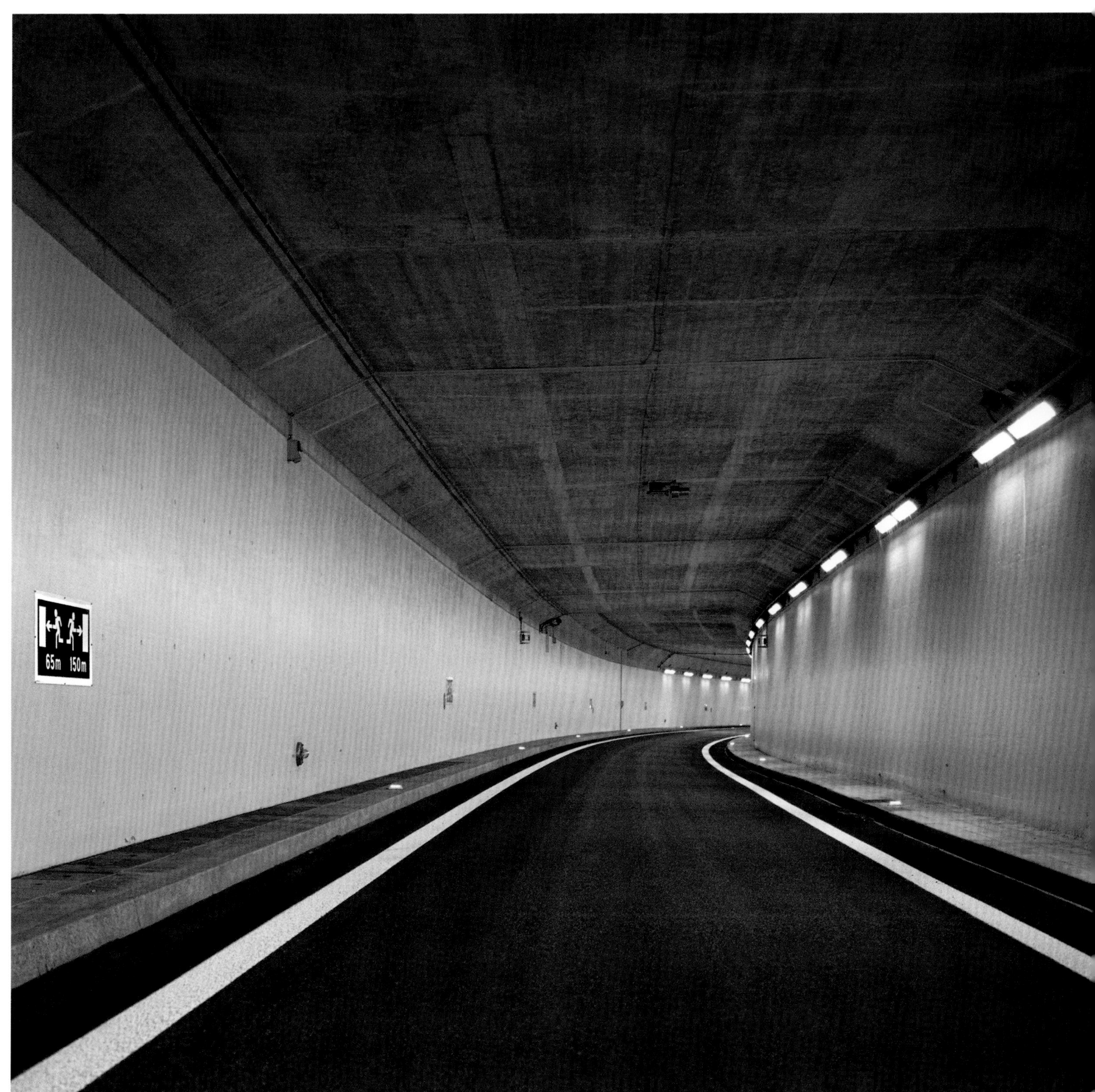
65m 150m

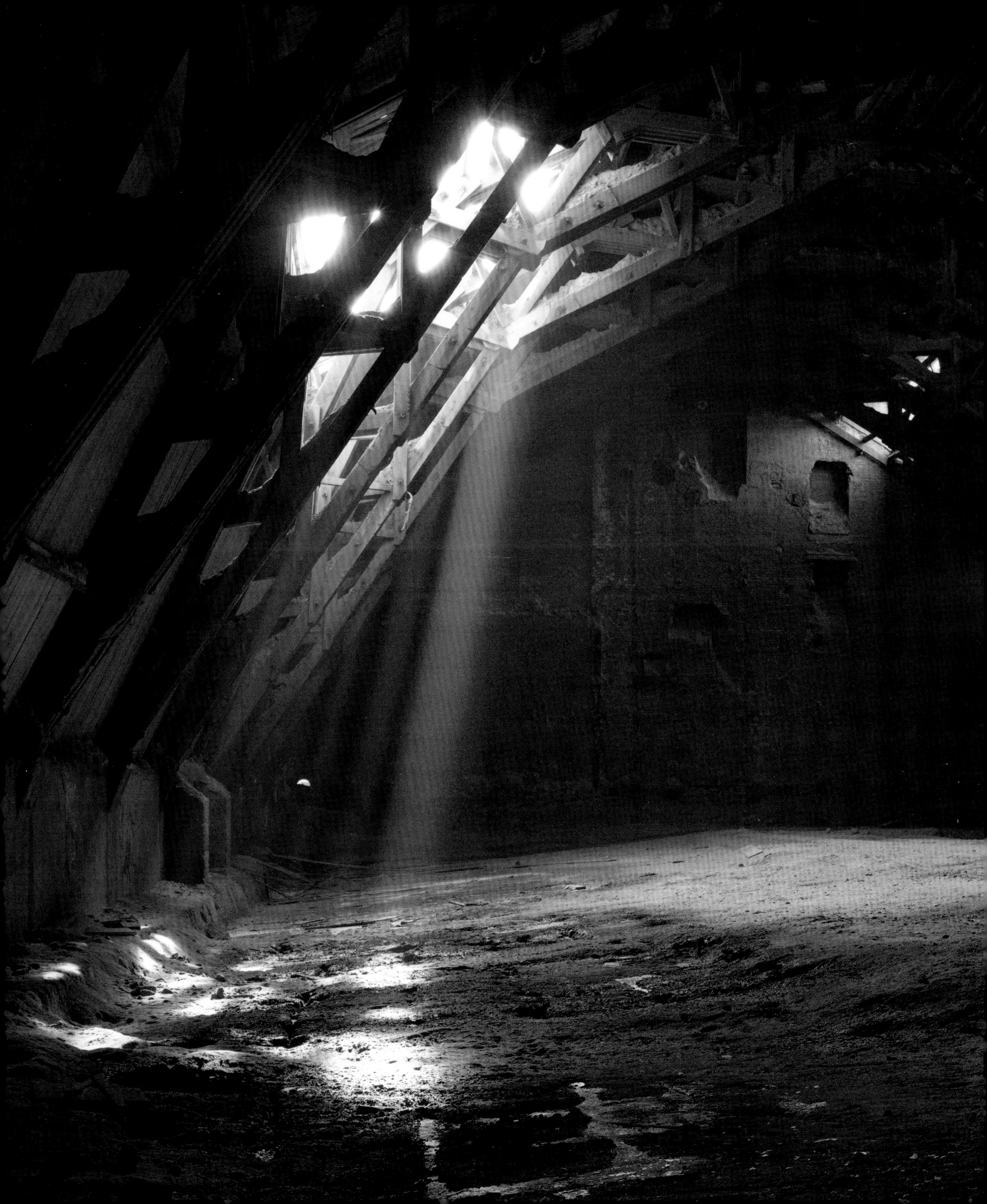

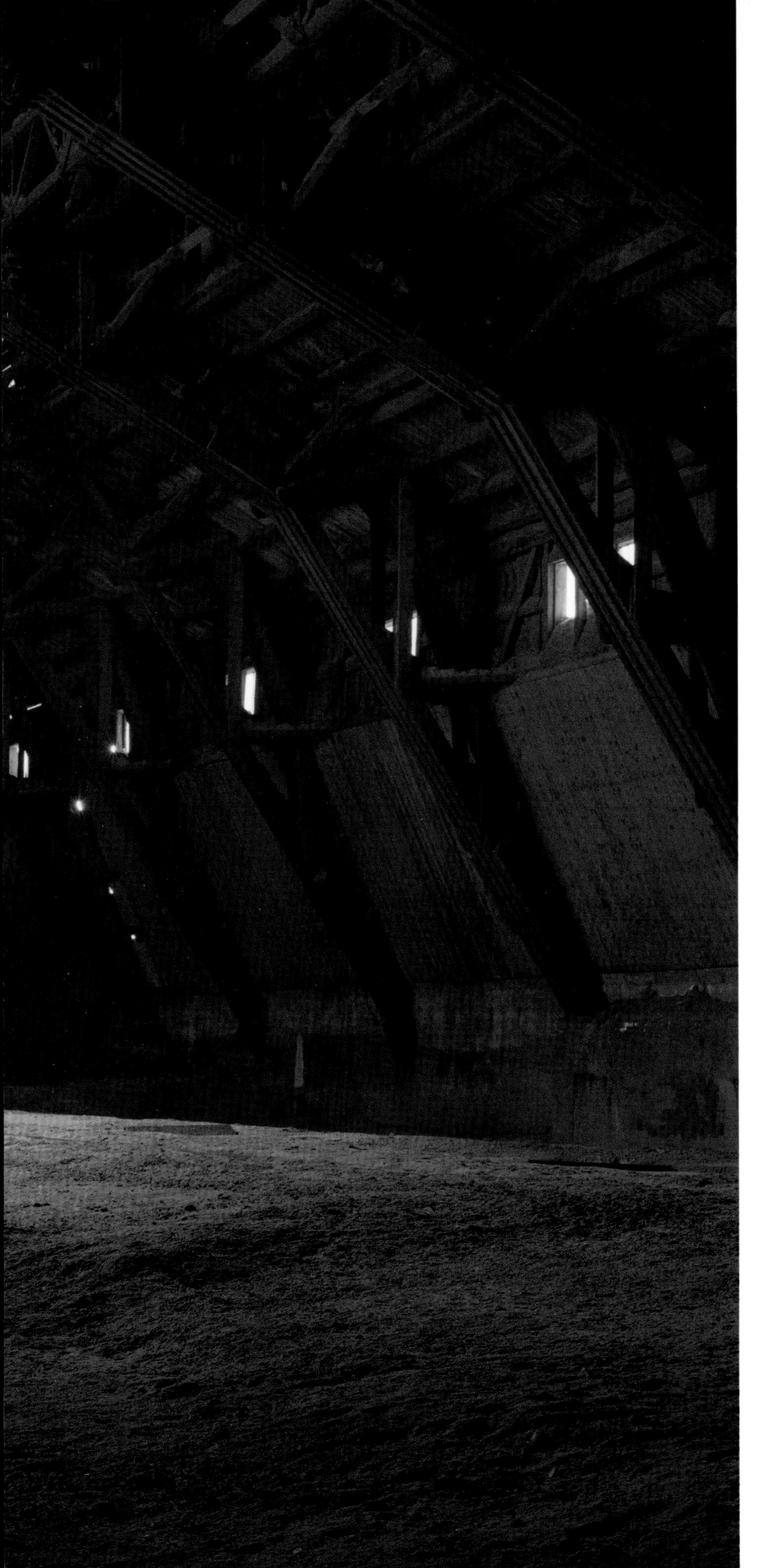

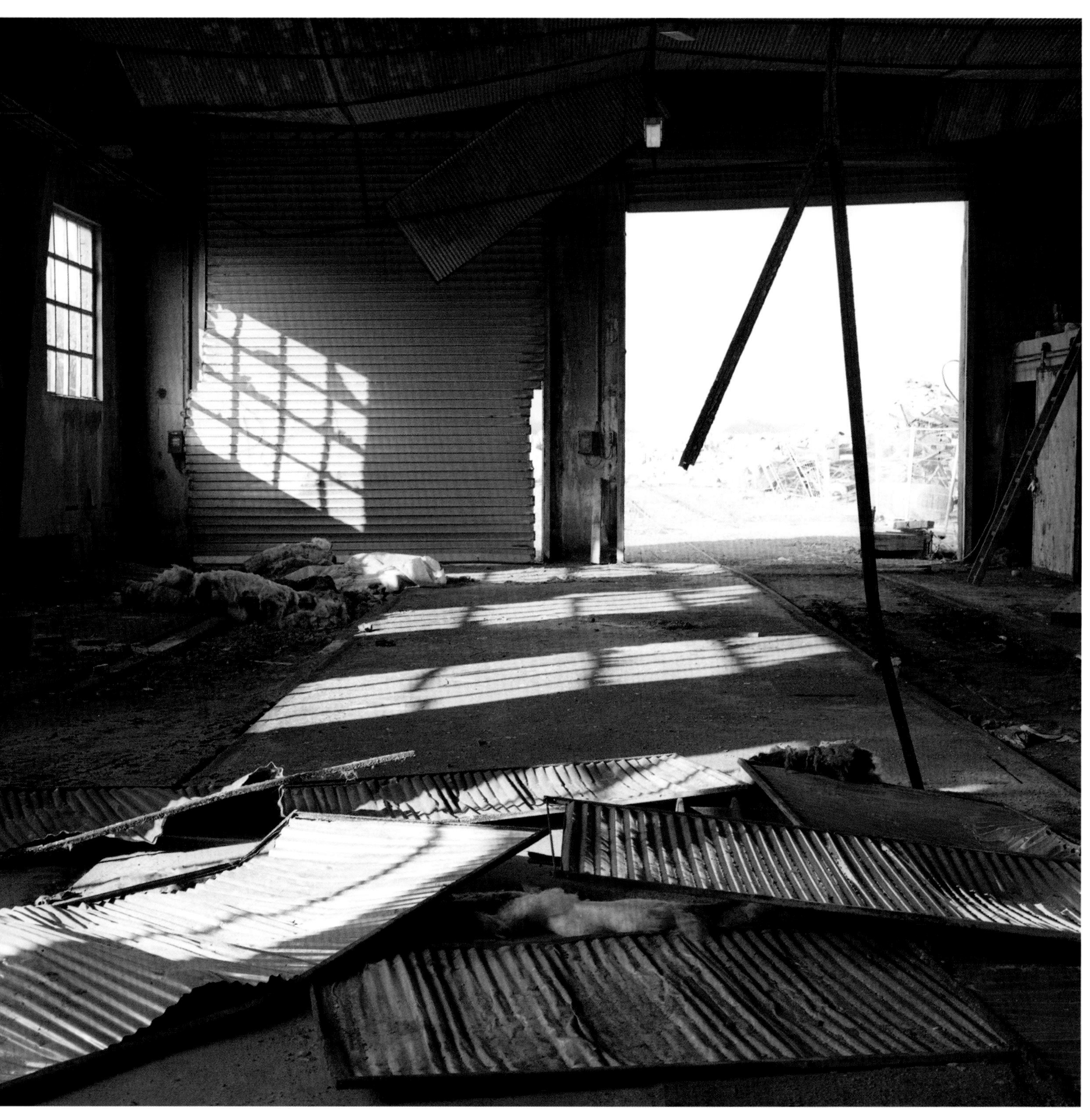

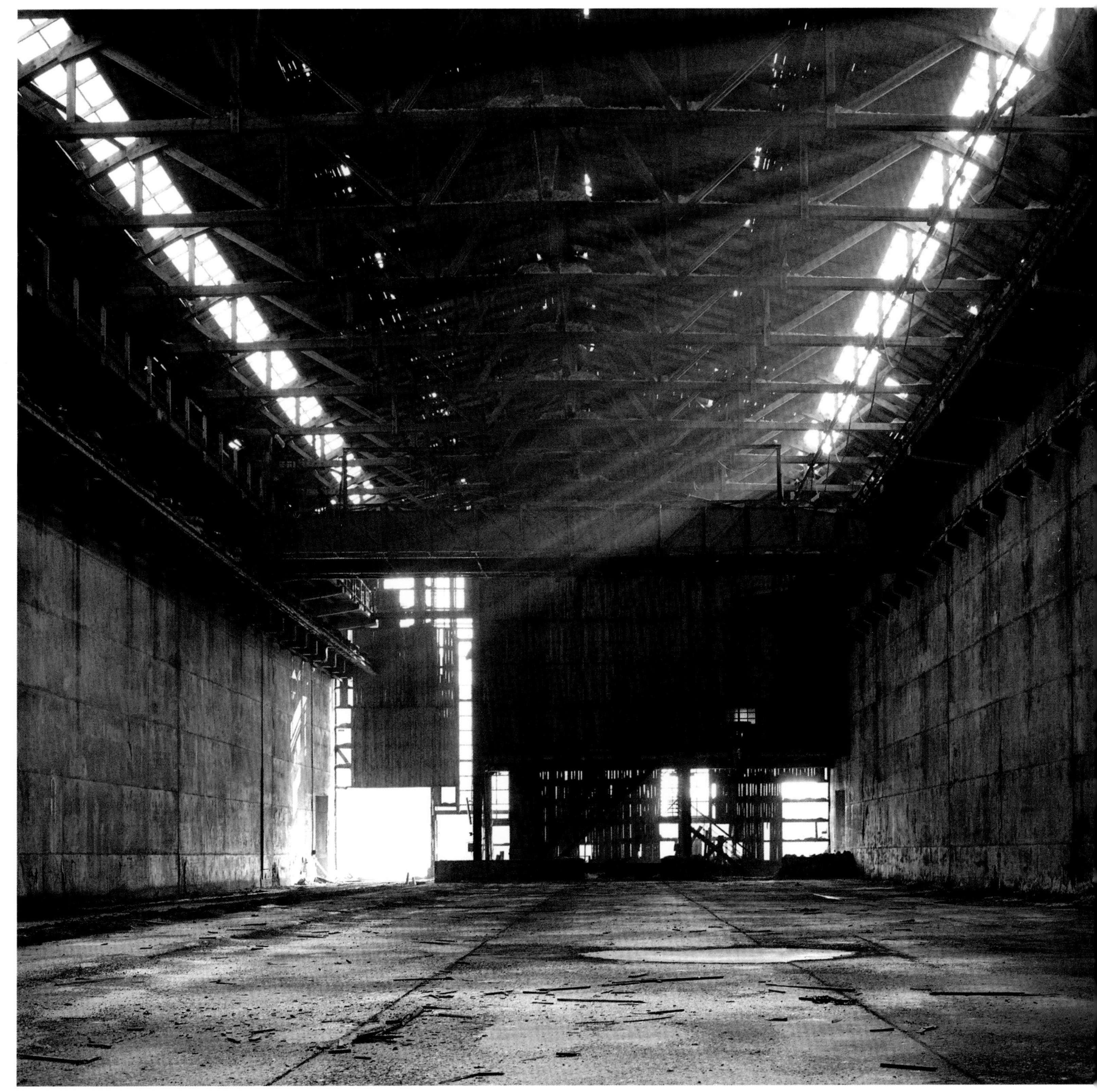

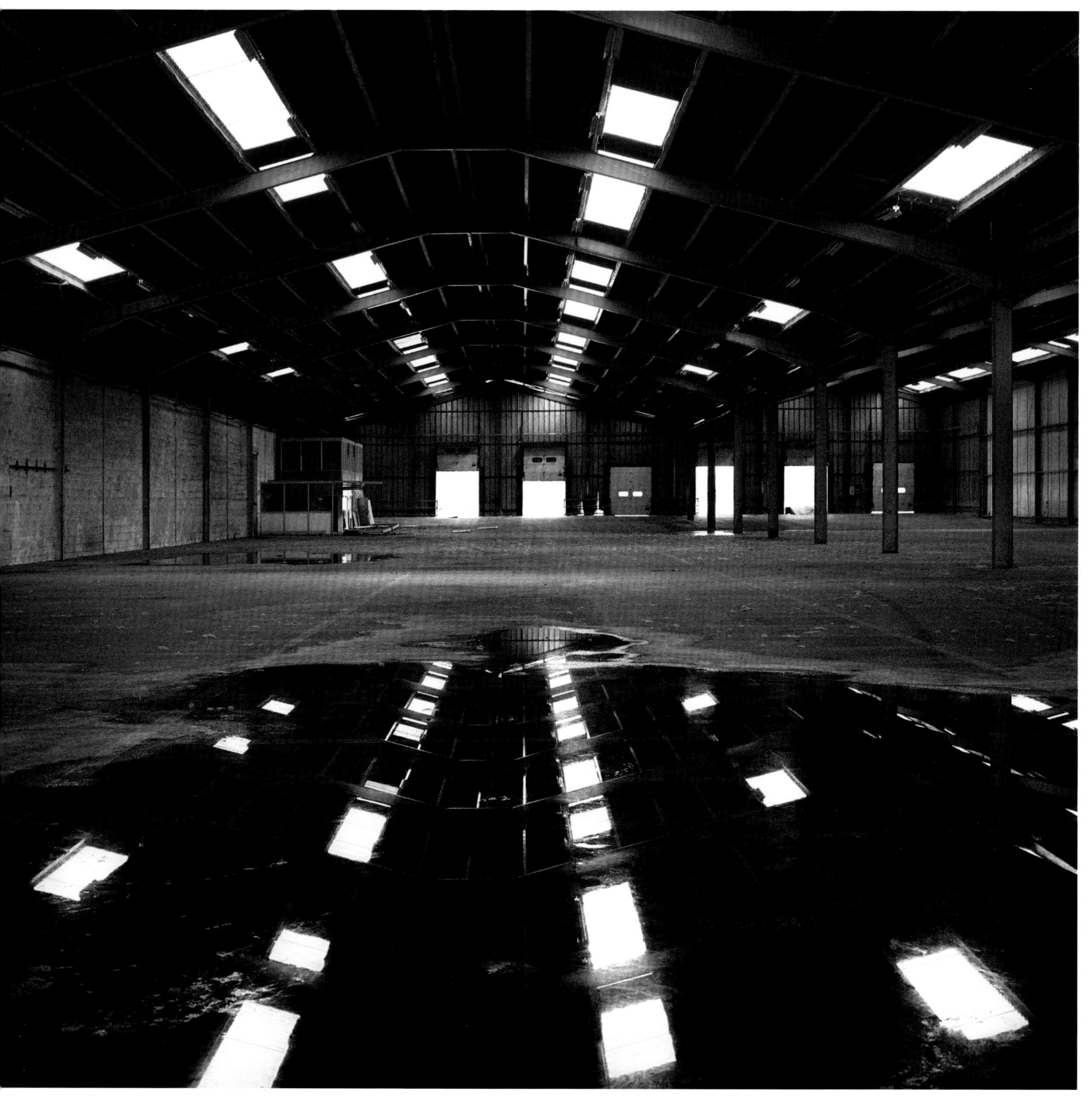

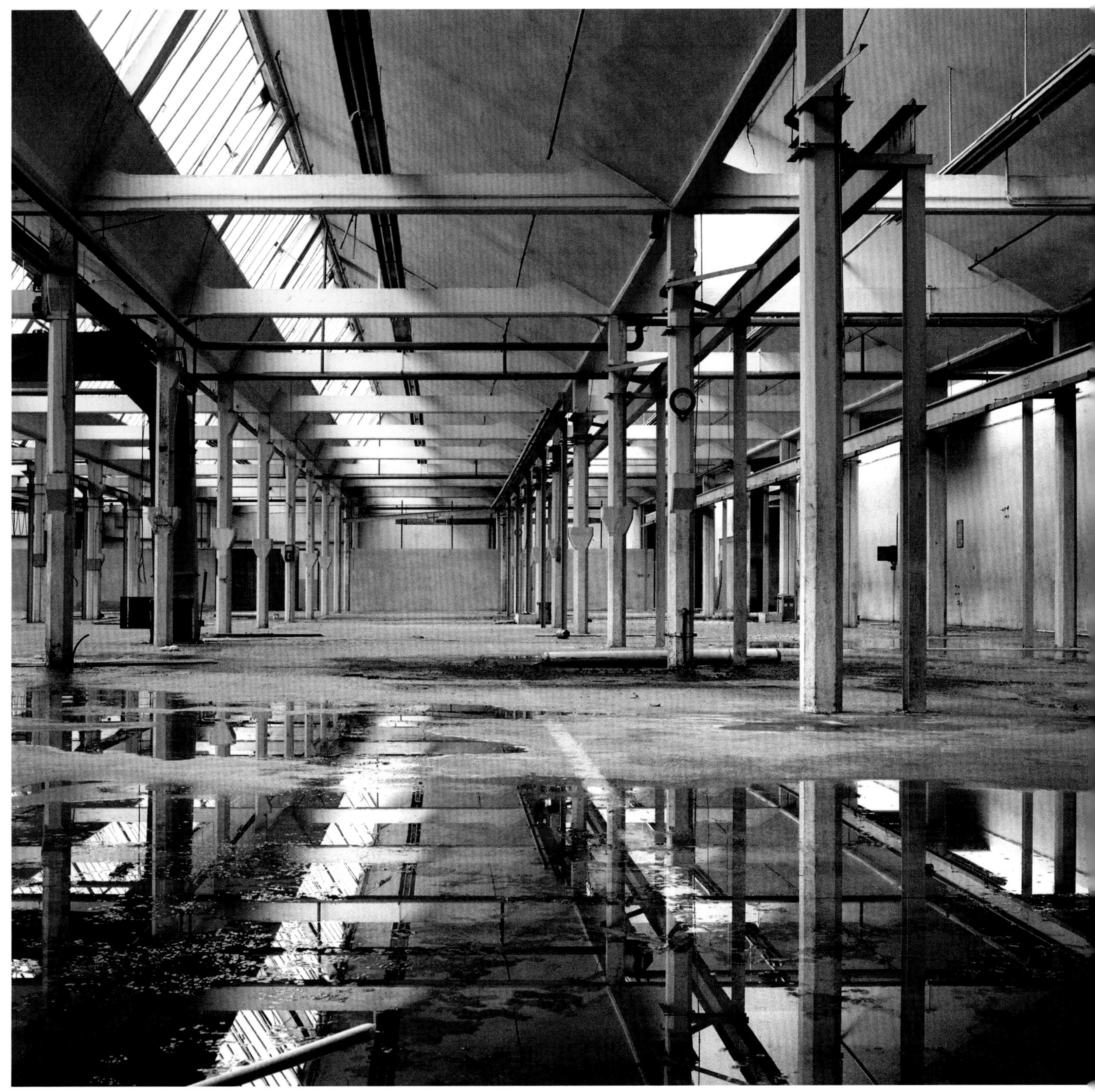

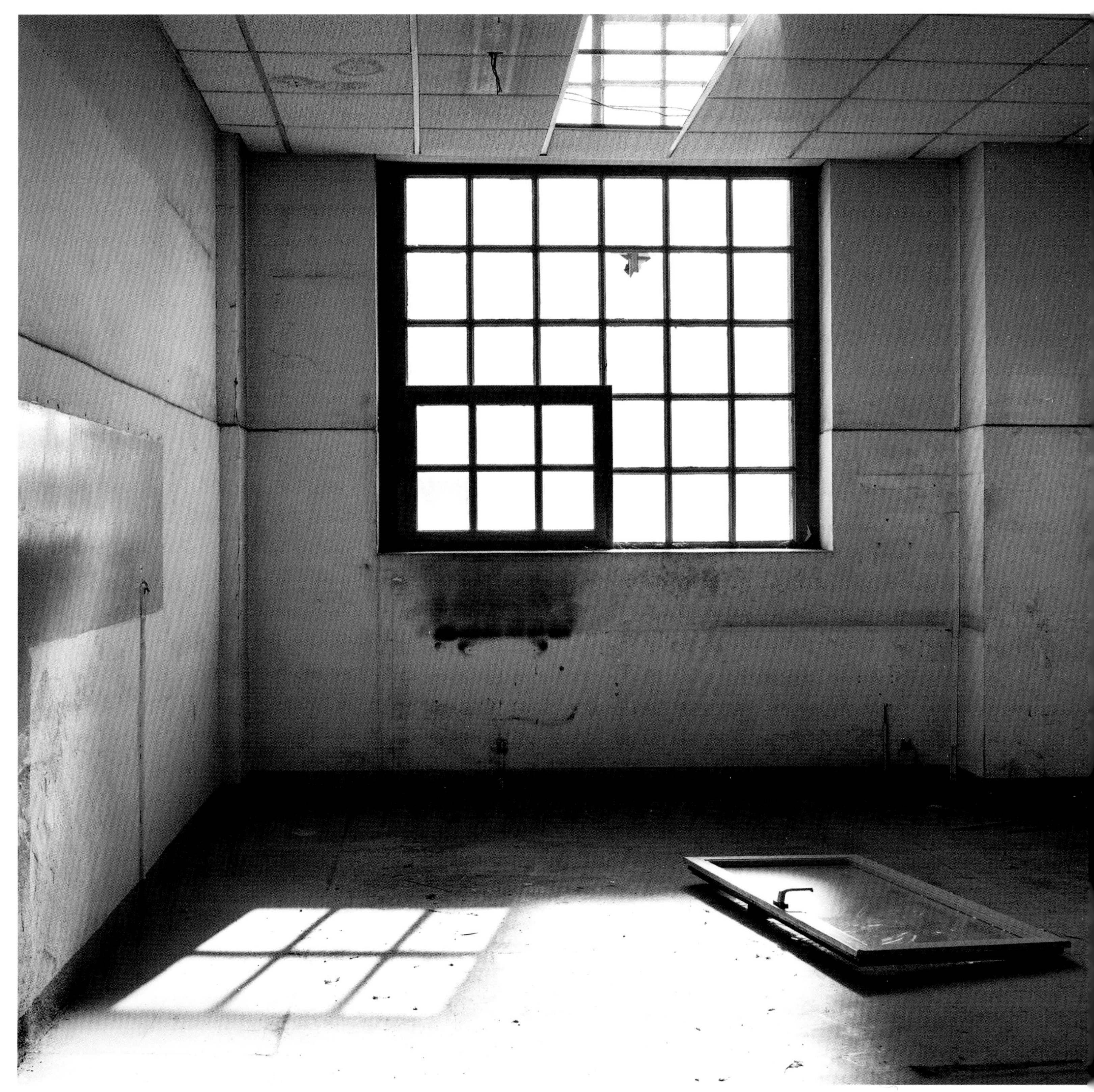

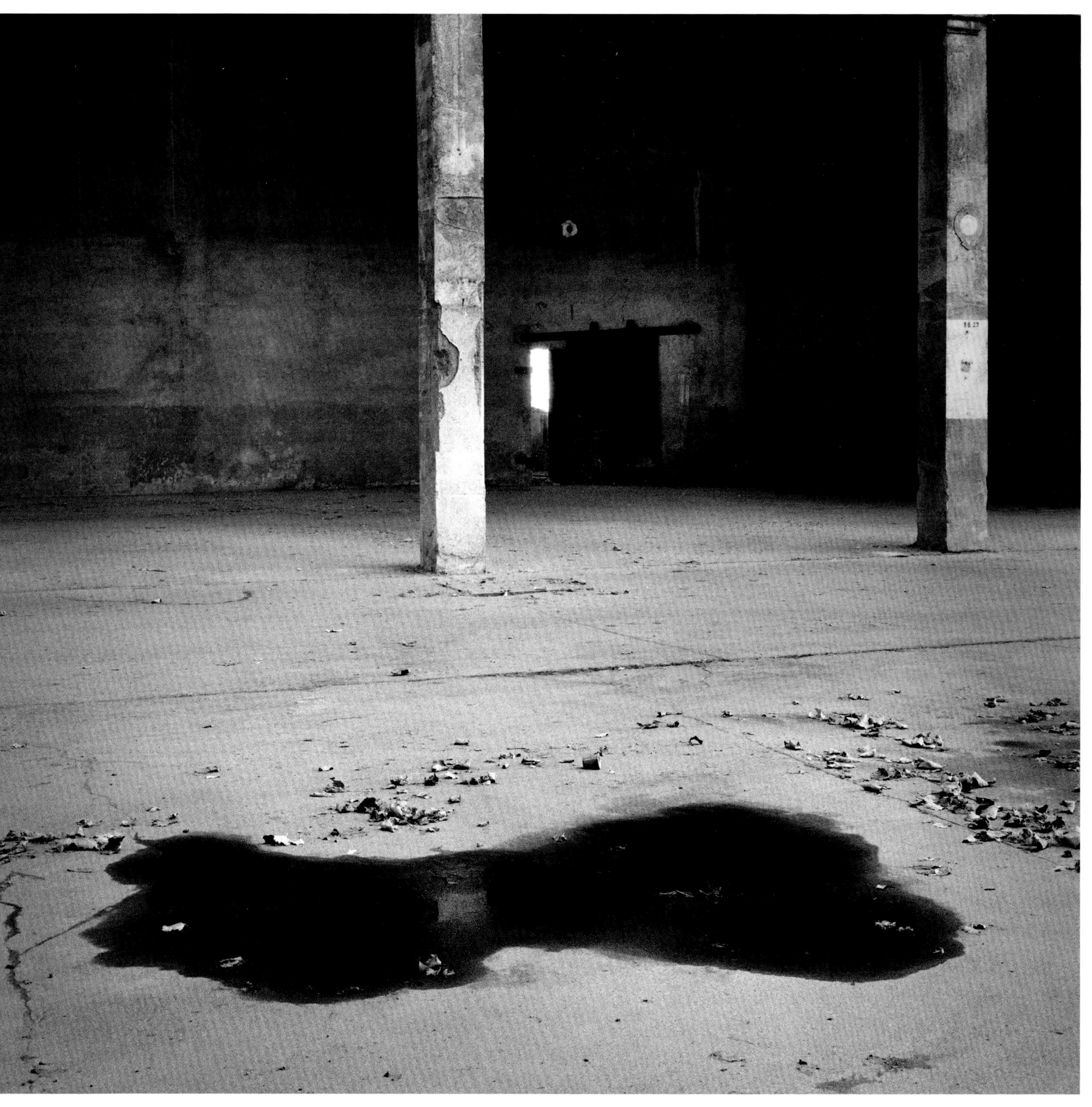

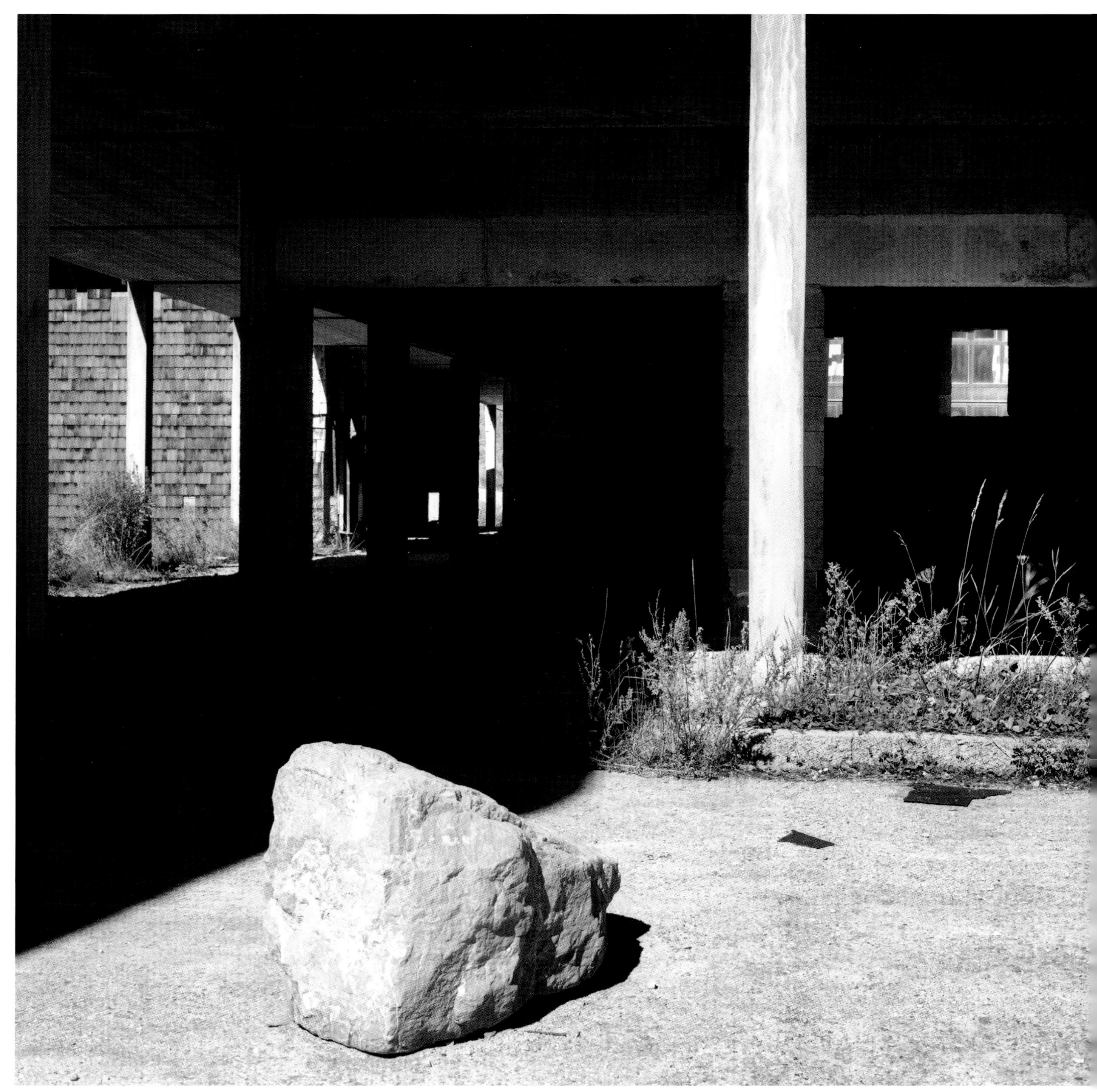

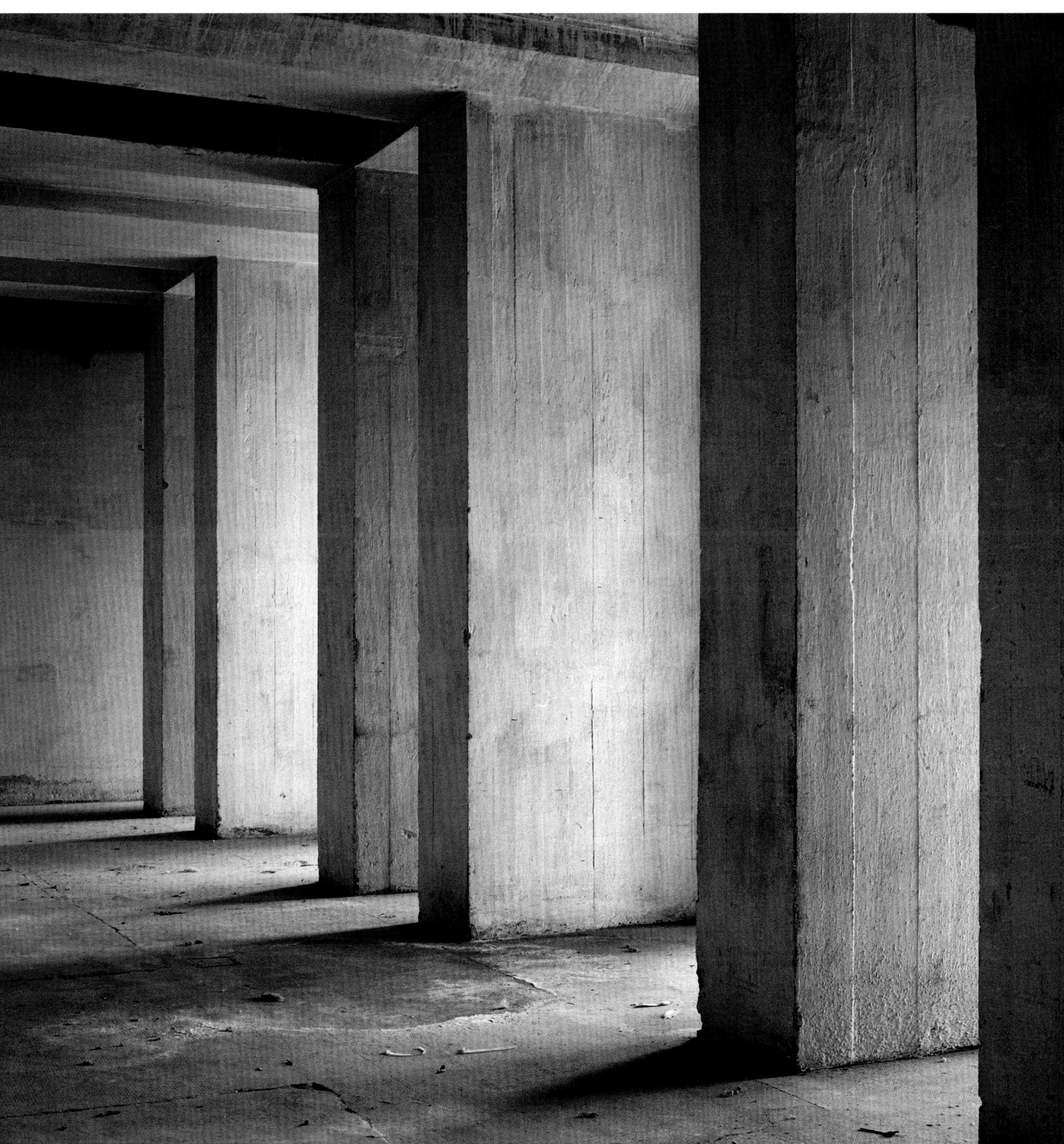

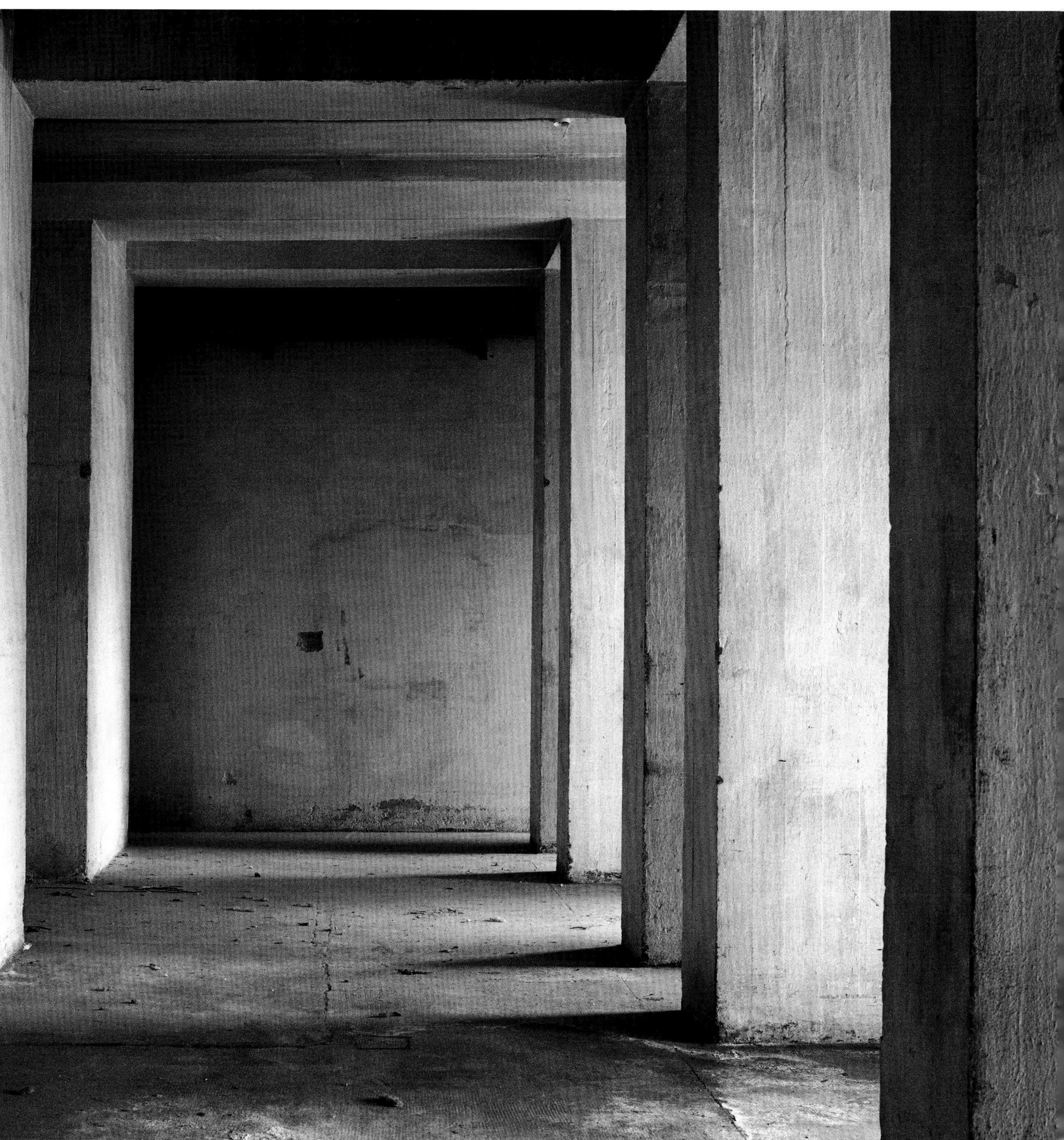

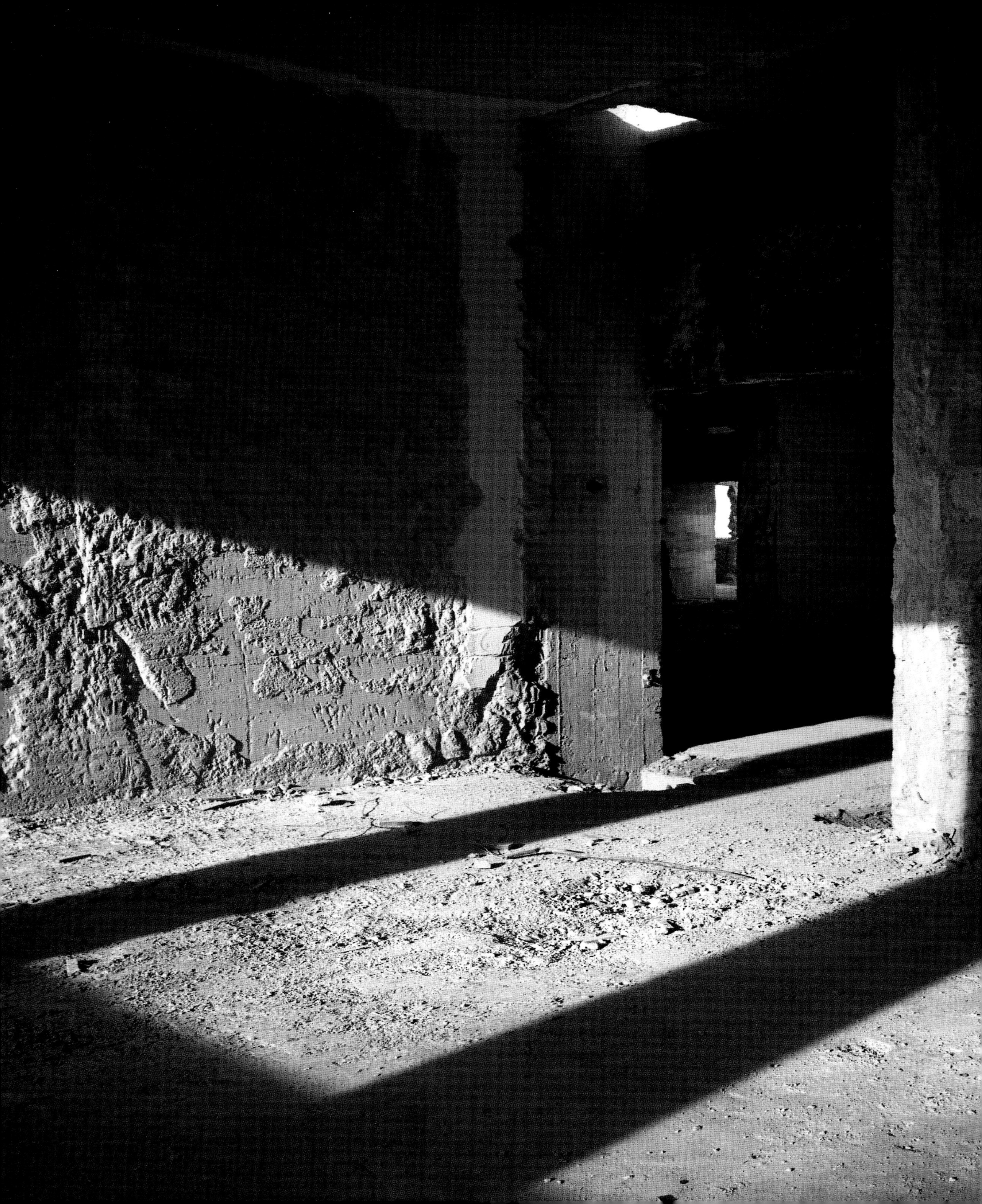

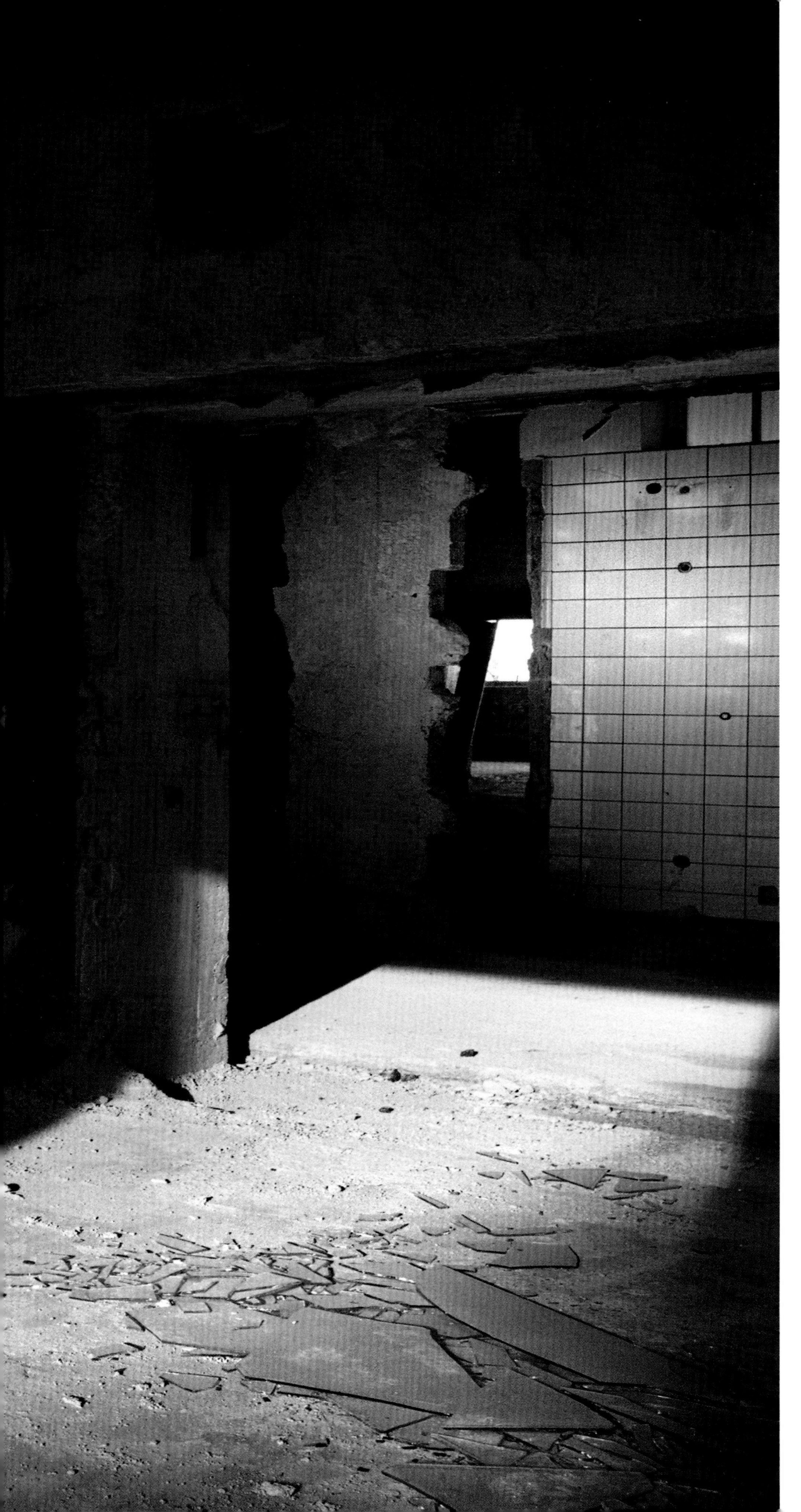

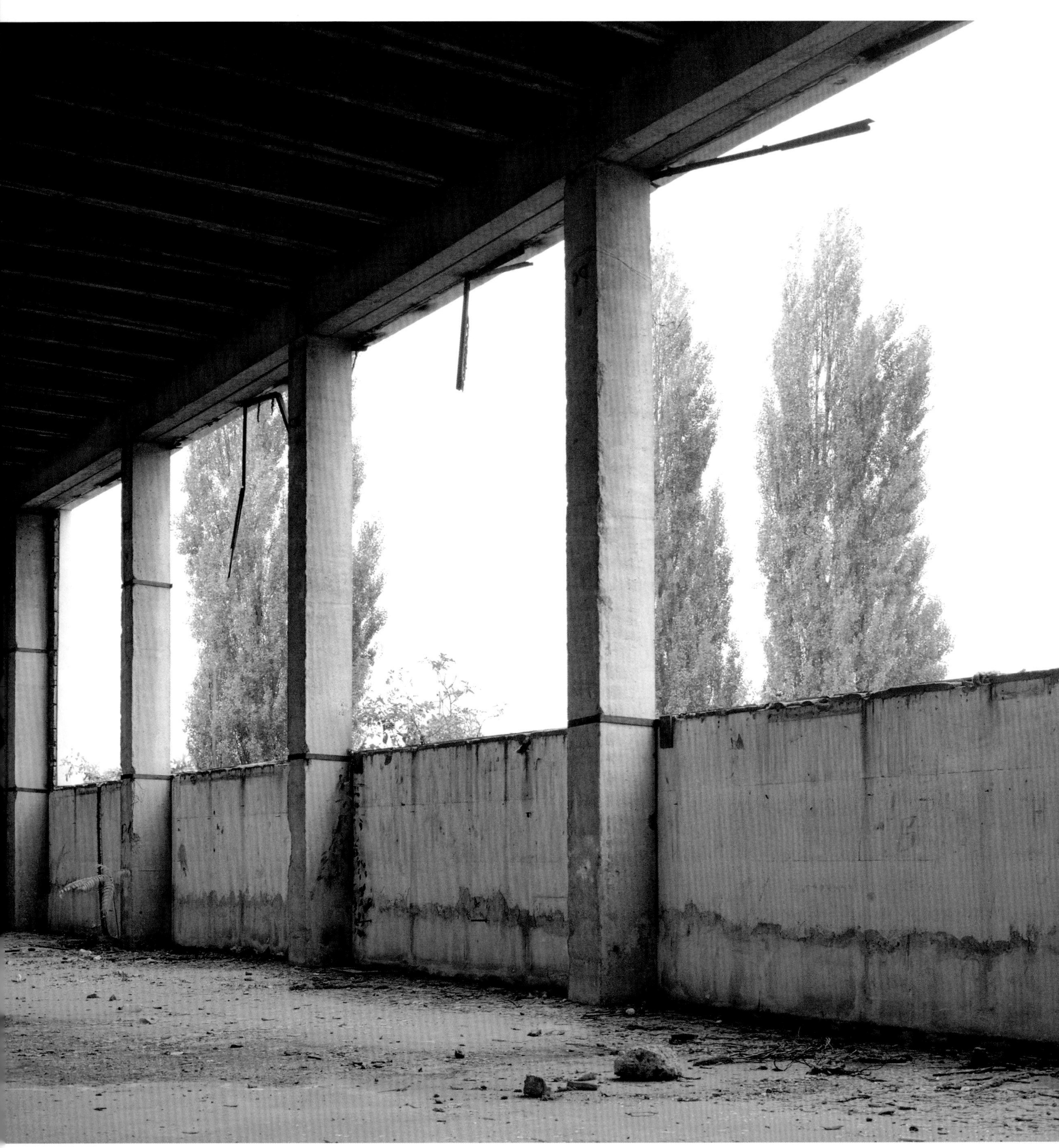

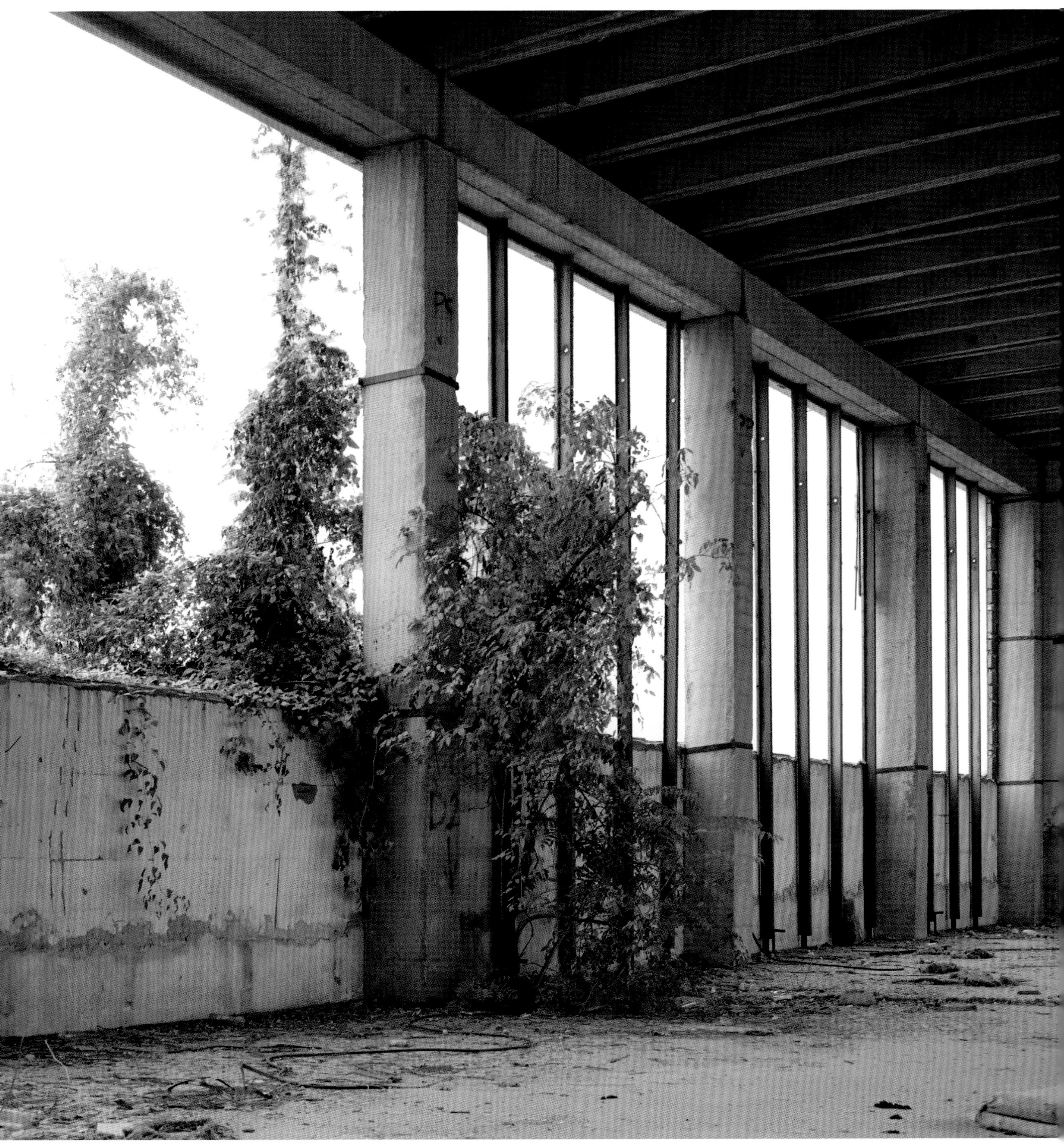

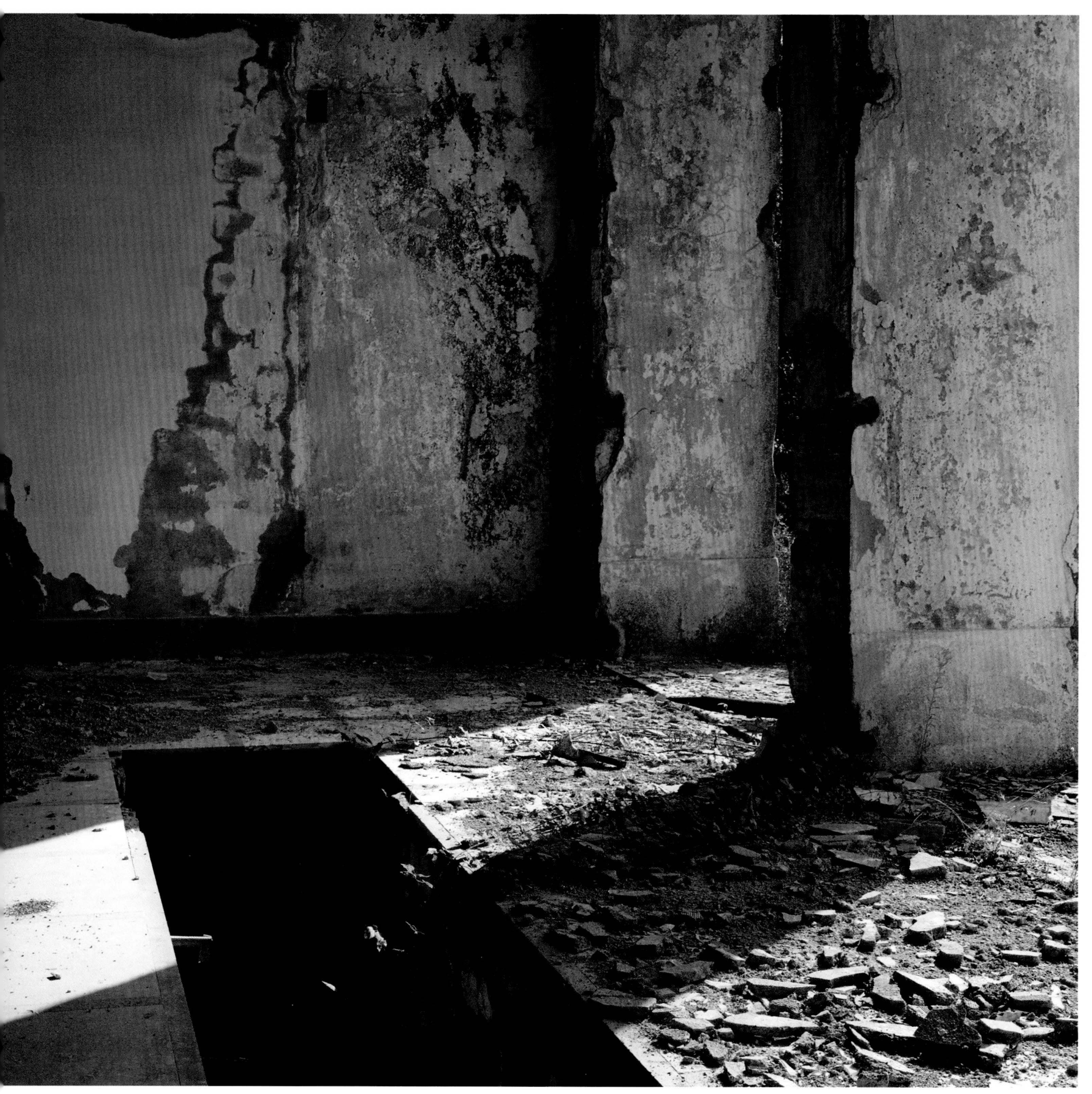

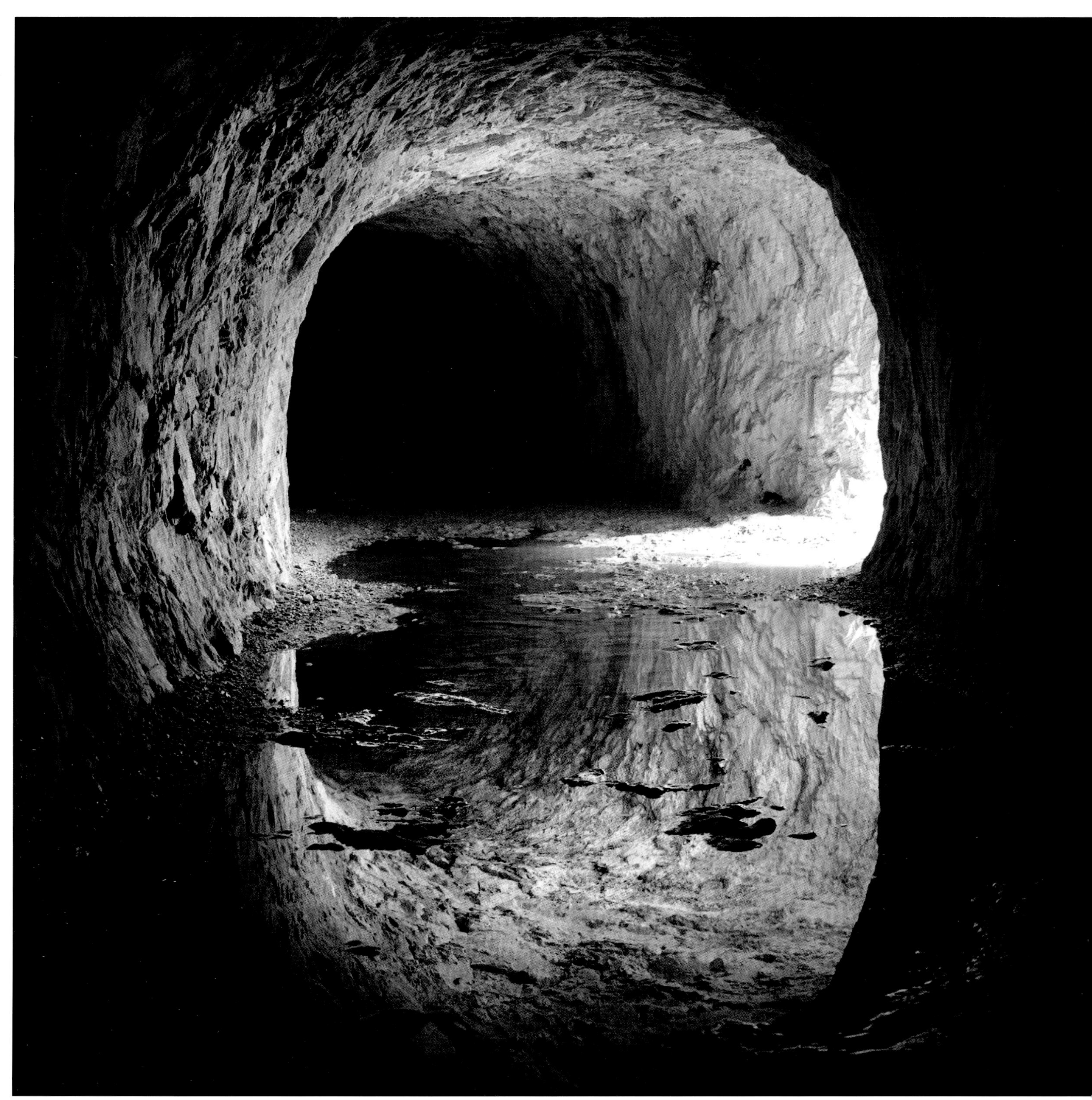

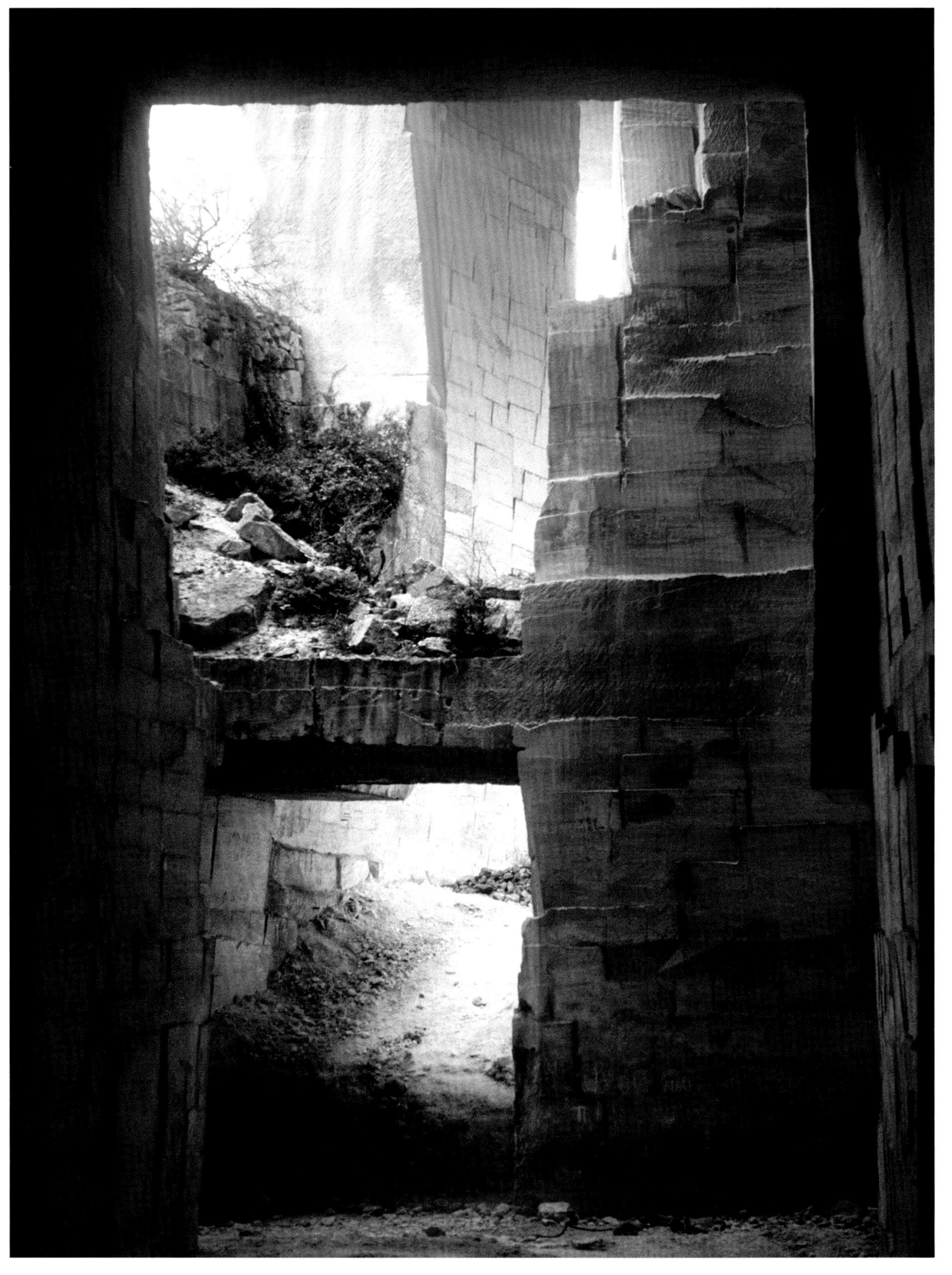

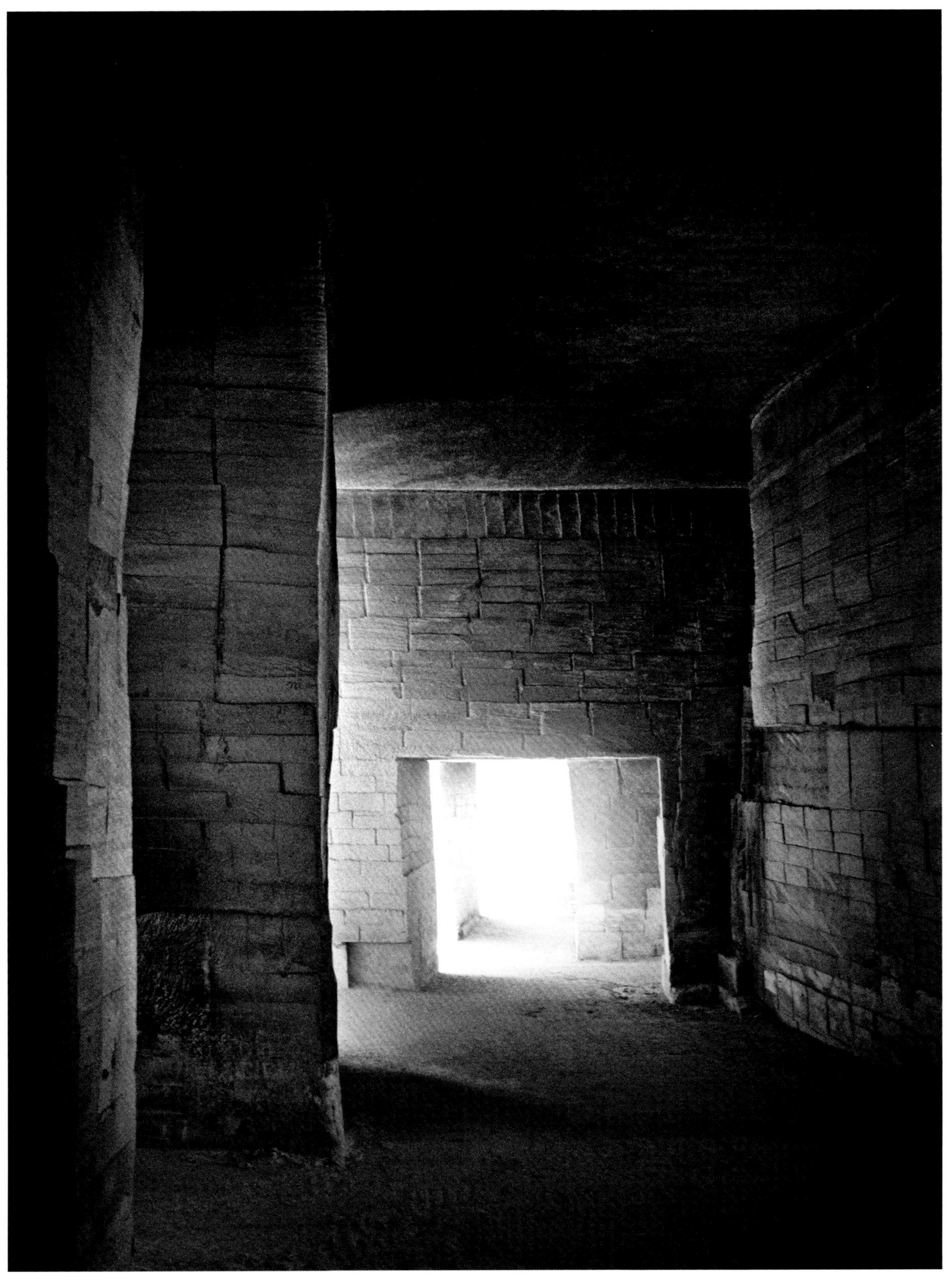

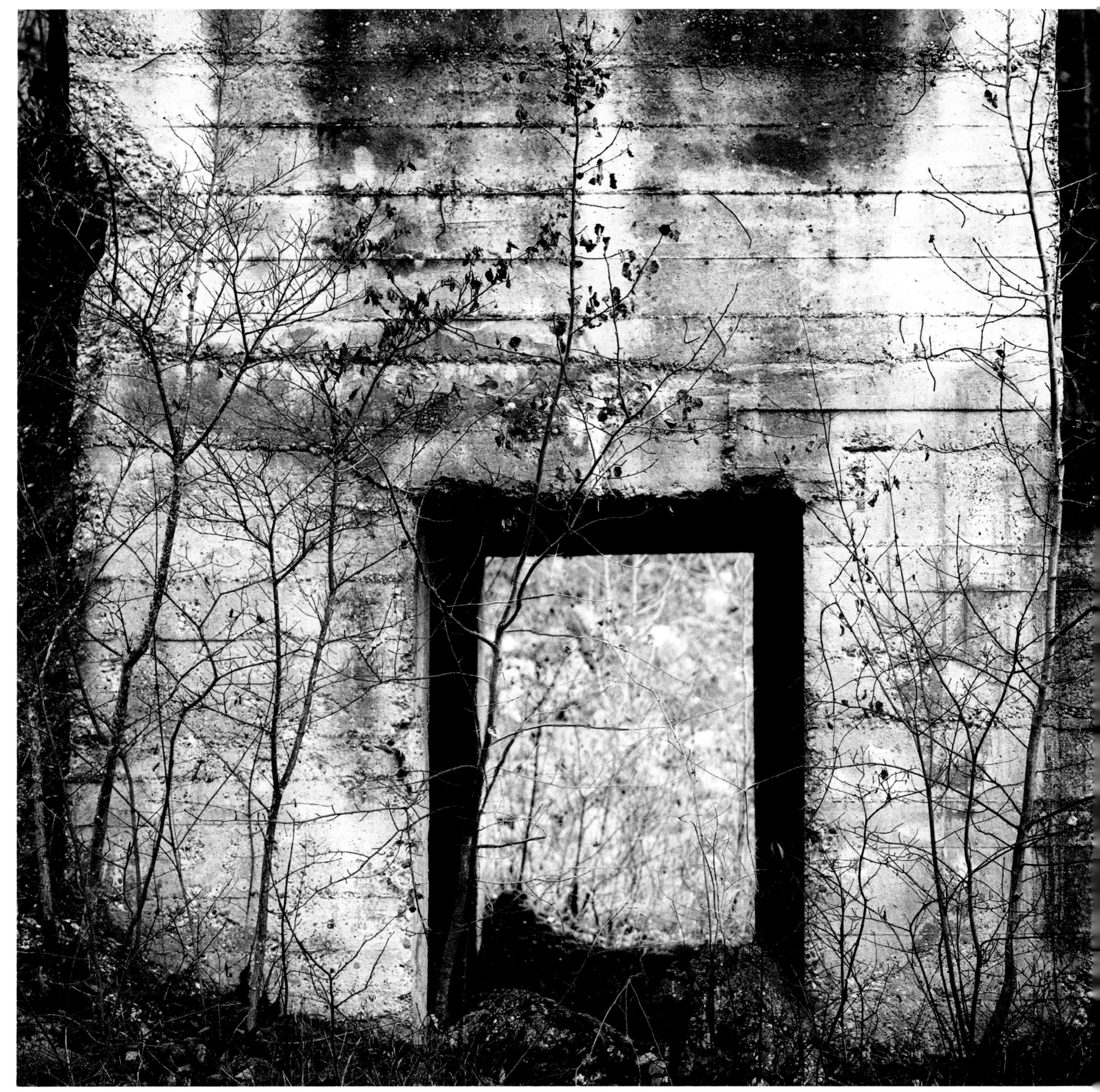

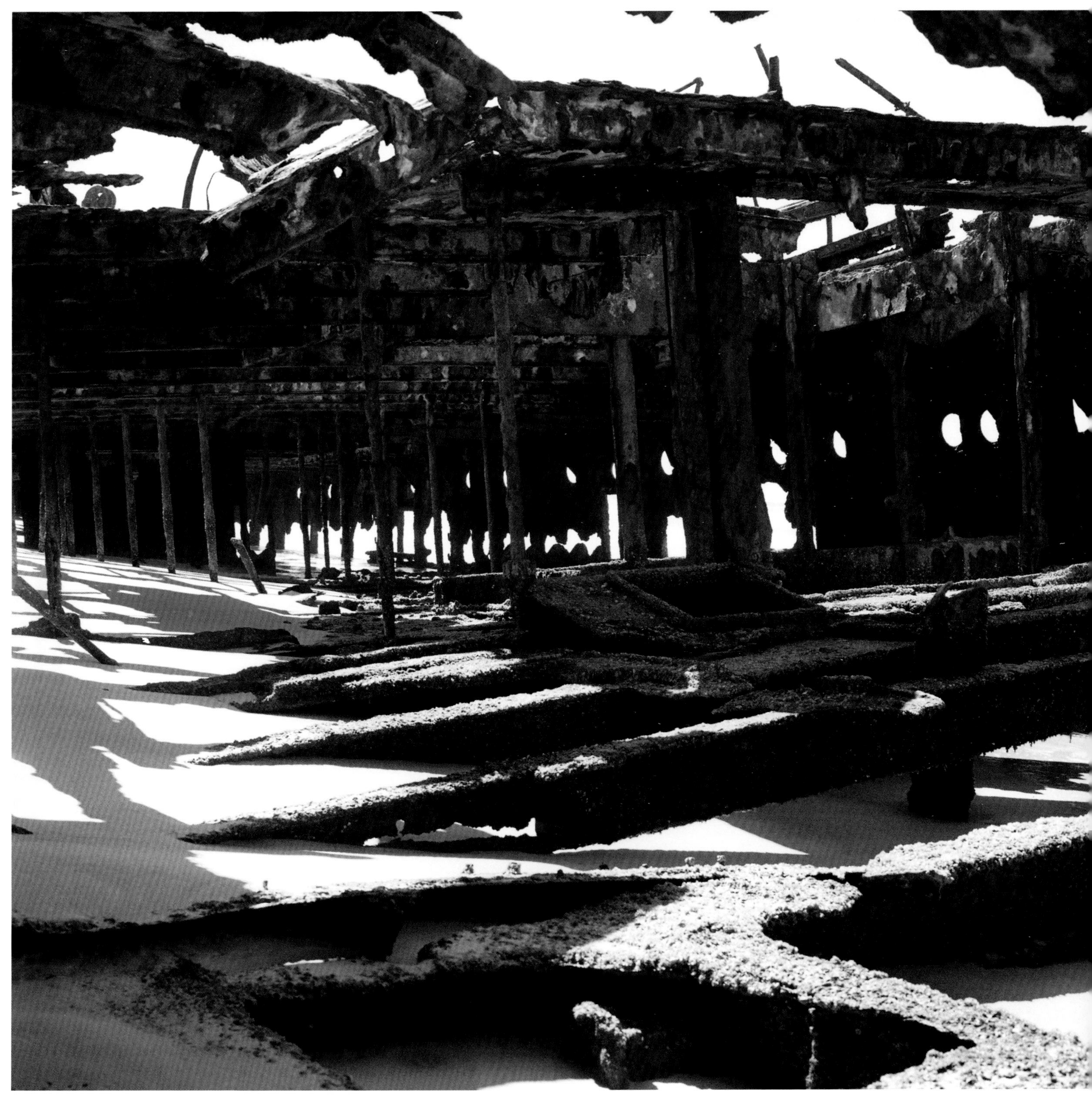

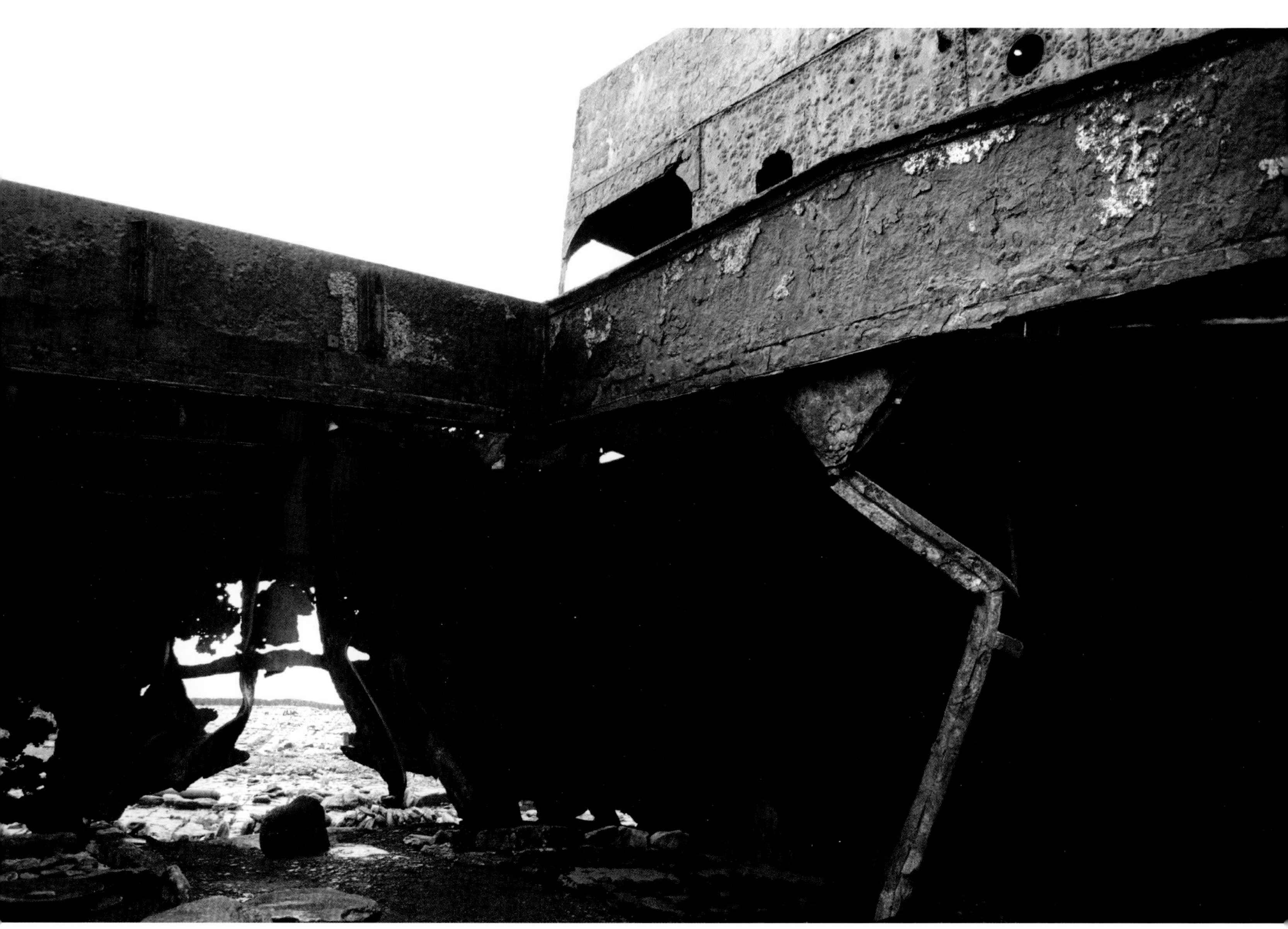

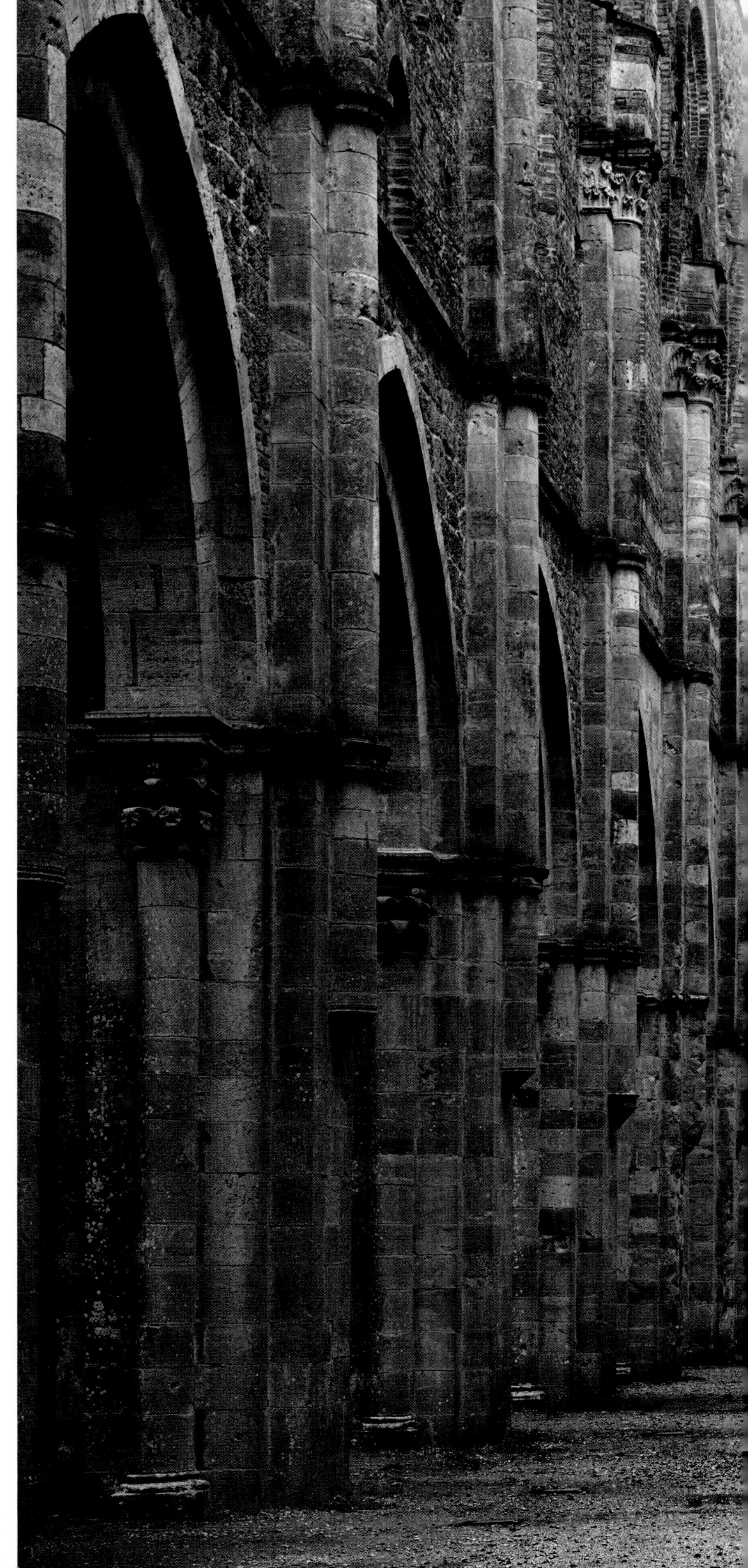

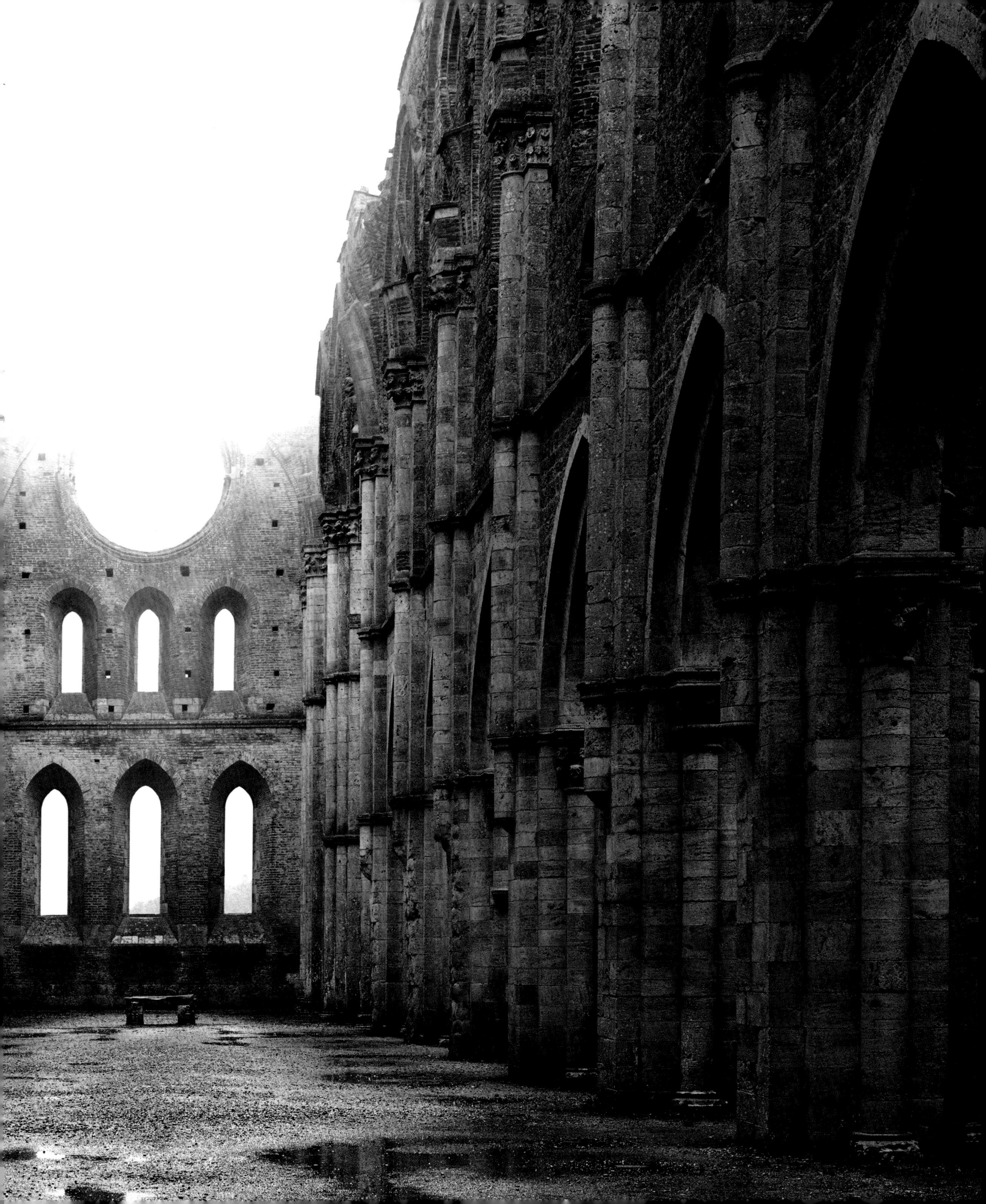

The tom cat had been watching over the ruins of the church of San Galgano near Siena for several years. In the 13th Century the cloister was a powerful and influential centre. From the 14th Century on the Cistercian abbey came under pressure from the plague, wars and political decisions. The roof of the nave collapsed and the site was converted into a farm. The picture of the church choir became well known through the film "Nostalghia" by Andrej Tarkovskij where the image of a simple, Russian timber house was superimposed onto it at the end of the film.

Na jedné z následujících stránek pozoruje kocour ruiny kostela San Galgano poblíž Sieny. Cisterciácký klášter byl ve třináctém století mocným a vlivným střediskem. Od čtrnáctého století se však stal obětí morových epidemií, válek a politických rozhodnutí. Střecha chrámové lodi se zřítila a kostel byl přebudován na statek. Obraz chrámového kůru se stal dobře známým poté, co zde Andrej Tarkovskij natočil svůj film „Nostalgie". Na konci filmu se obraz tohoto kůru pomalu prolíná s obrazem omšelé ruské roubené chalupy.

Der Kater bewachte mehrere Jahre lang die Ruine der Kirche San Galgano bei Siena. Das Kloster war im 13. Jahrhundert ein mächtiges und einflussreiches Zentrum. Bereits ab dem 14. Jahrhundert litt die Zisterzienserabtei unter dem Druck von Pest, Kriegen und politischen Entscheidungen. Das Dach des Kirchenschiffes fiel ein und die Anlage wurde zu einem Bauernhof umgestaltet. Das Bild des Kirchenchores ist bekannt geworden durch den Film "Nostalghia" von Andrej Tarkovskij, wo es am Schluss des Filmes vom Bild eines einfachen russischen Holzhauses überblendet wird.

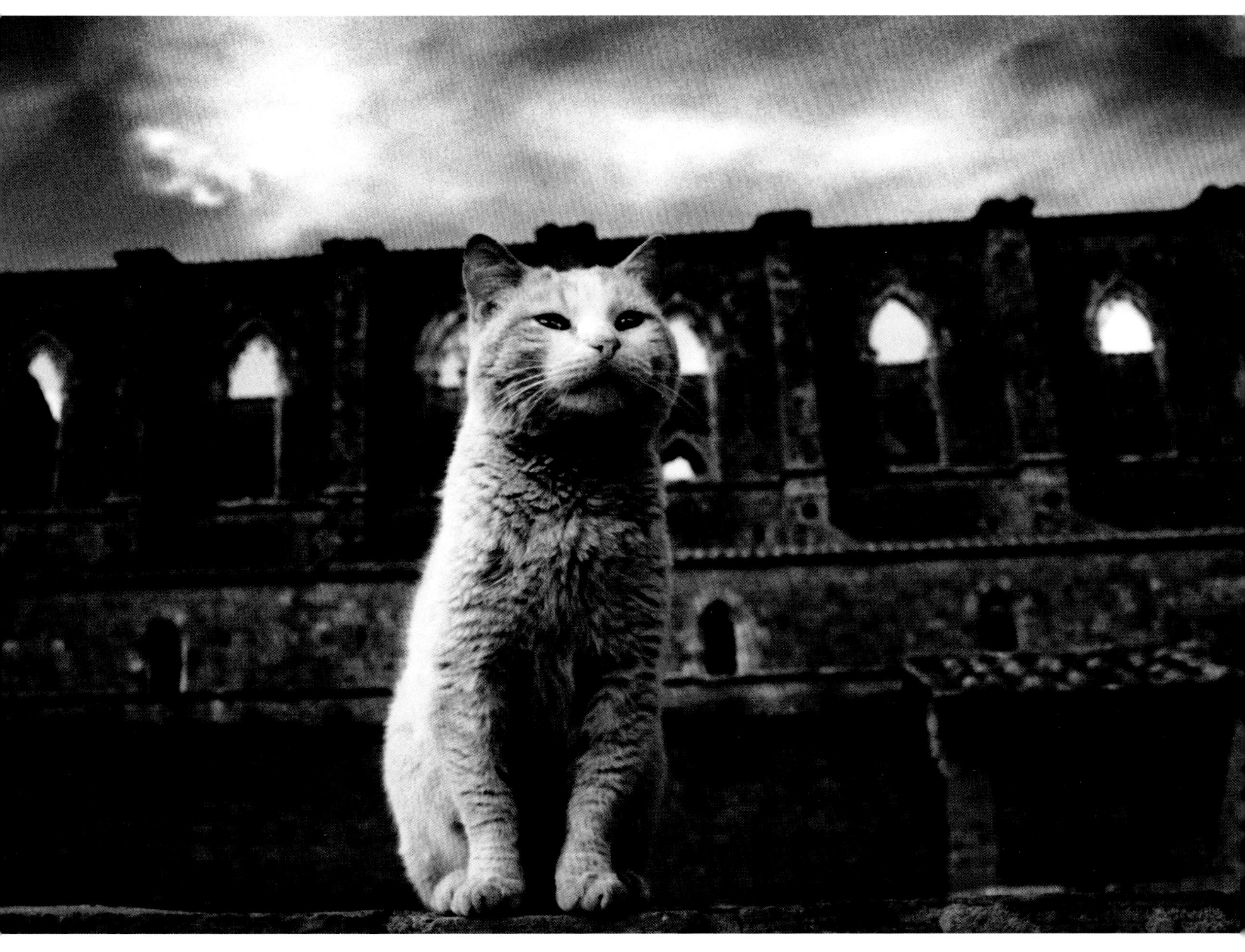

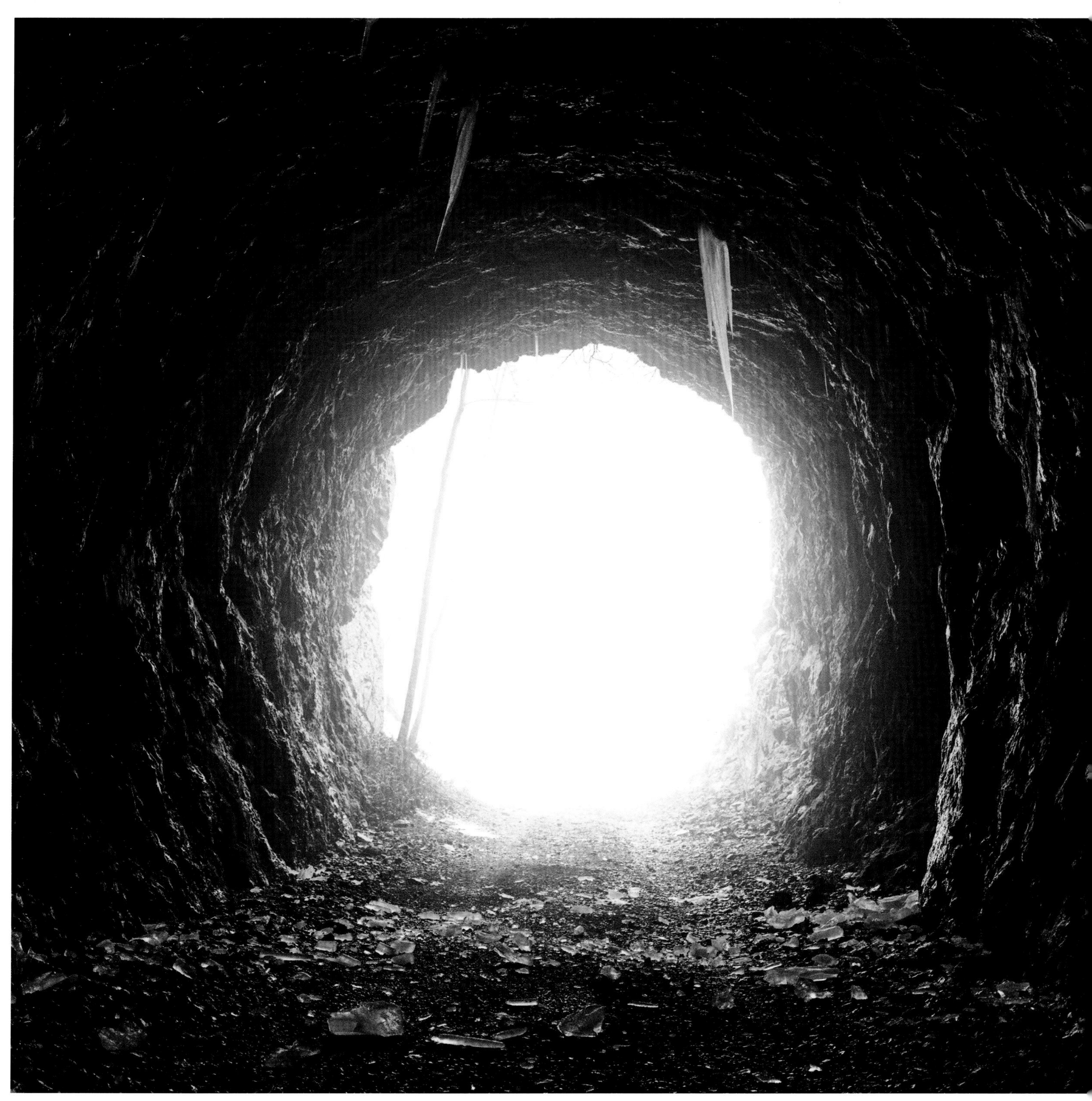

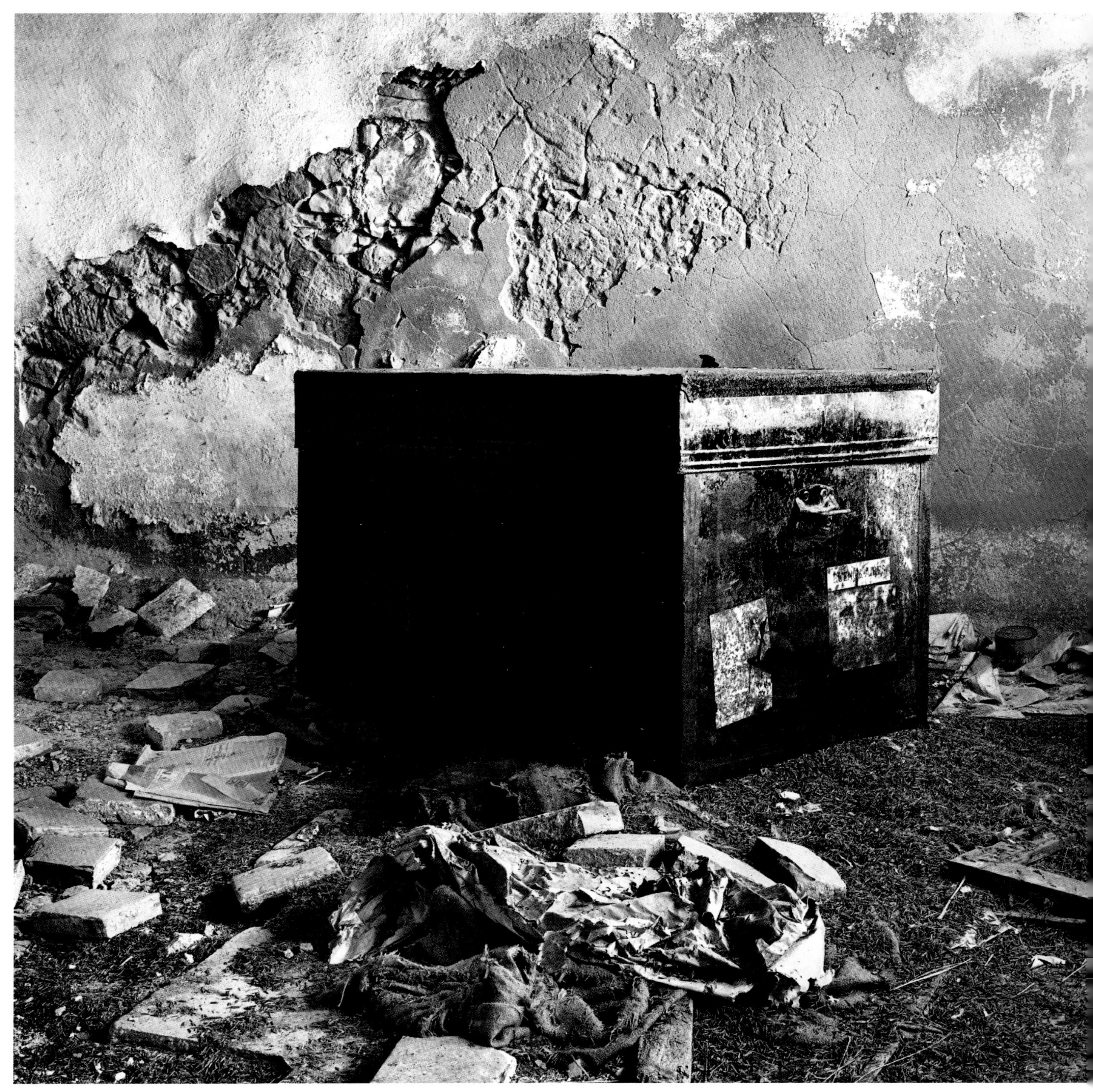

List of Photographs

61 Roadwork; Delémont, Switzerland; 2003
63 Roadwork; Moutier, Switzerland; 2007
65 Roadwork; Delémont, Switzerland; 2003
67 Roadwork; Moutier, Switzerland; 2007
69 Tunnel; Münchenstein, Switzerland; 2006
70 Highway-tunnel; Basel, Switzerland; 2006
71 Highway-tunnel; Basel, Switzerland; 2006
72 Salt mine; Mulhouse, France; 2000
74 Salt mine; Mulhouse, France; 2003
75 Salt mine; Mulhouse, France; 2003
76 Factory; Arles, France; 2006
77 Chemical plant; Huningue, France; 2007
79 Salt mine; Mulhouse, France; 2001
80 Factory, Arles, France; 2006
81 Garage; Col de Larche, Italy; 1999
83 Chemical plant; Pratteln, Switzerland; 2007
84 Chemical plant; Basel, Switzerland; 2010
87 Factory; Bratislava, Slovakia; 2005
88 Factory; Grosseto, Italy; 1997
89 Tunnel; Gorge du Verdon, France; 2008
90 Limestone quarry; Les Baux-de-Provence, France; 1979
91 Limestone quarry; Les Baux-de-Provence, France; 1979
93 Limestone quarry; Leymen, France; 2006
95 Shipwreck; Fraser Island, Australia; 2006
97 Shipwreck; Aran Islands, Ireland; 1994
99 Abbey; San Galgano, Tuscany, Italy; 2000
101 Tom cat; San Galgano, Tuscany, Italy; 1990
102 Passage of the comet Hale-Bopp; Switzerland; 1997
105 Tunnel; Erschwil, Switzerland; 2010
107 Overseas trunk; Grosseto, Tuscany, Italy, 1998
110 Bunker; Praha, Czech Republic; 2011

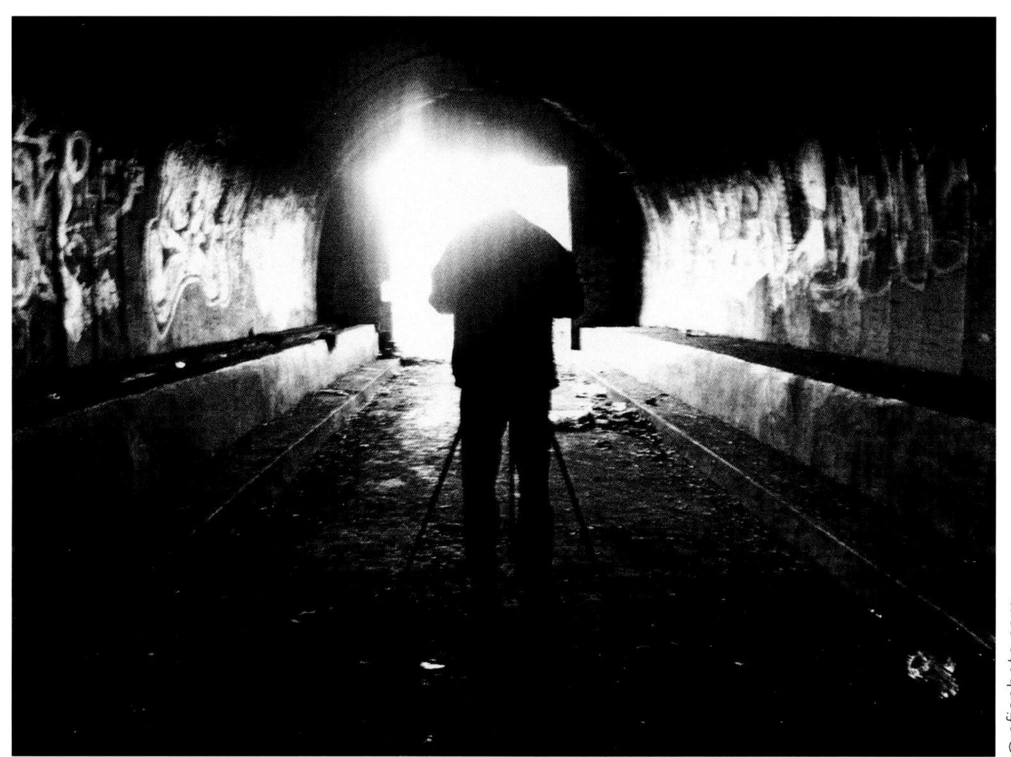

Erwin Staeheli (b. 1955) studied art in Basel, Switzerland from 1974 to 1977. He focused first on painting then later specialised in photography. Between 1980 and 1994 he also worked as a civil engineer, planning and supervising road works, concrete and steel construction, waste water treatment and water supply. Since 1995 he has worked exclusively as an art photographer, preferring to use medium and large format cameras, printing the old fashioned way in his own laboratory on fibre-based papers.

The master-copies of most of the photographs are silver-gelatine prints on fibre-based paper, approx. 40x40 cm (16"x16") and 40x50 cm (16"x20").

"passage" is part of the main work "triptych" that also includes the series "promenade" and "transformation".

66 photographs about a Jurassic journey in Switzerland and France have been published in the book "exposé". ISBN: 978-3-7965-2233-8. Delivered by Schwabe AG, 4132 Muttenz, Switzerland.

List of the solo-exhibitions:
Galerie FotoGrafic, Prague, Czech Republic, 2010
Galerie Monika Wertheimer, Oberwil, Switzerland, 2009
Gallery Tosei-sha, Tokyo, Japan, 2009
Instituto Cultural de México, San Antonio, Fotoseptiembre USA, 2009
Galerie Fiducia, Ostrava, Czech Republic, 2008
Galerie Pep+No Name, Basel, Switzerland, 2001-2008
L'Atelier, lieu d'art visuel, Apt, France, 2006
Galerie G4, Cheb, Czech Republic, 2006

Updated information about the art-work, publishing, exhibitions and contact: www.winpic.ch

Many thanks to Alena Dvořáková and Viktor Fischer for their support.

PASSAGE
erwin staeheli

Photographs / Fotografie: Erwin Staeheli / -win © 2011
Text: Erwin Staeheli
Graphic design / Grafika: Vladimir Vimr and Martin Vimr
Translators / Překlad: Jiří Fojtek, Anna Ball, Eberhard Pfleiderer
Language editing: Richard Škvařil
Litography: KANT
Printing and binding: PB tisk Příbram (Czech Republic)
Published by / Vydal: KANT, Karel Kerlický, 2011, kant@kant-books.com

ISBN: 978-80-7437-058-8